INVESTING YOUR
NEST EGG

D1445540

A SENSIBLE APPROACH TO
BUILDING A PROFITABLE PORTFOLIO
IN THE NEW GOLDEN AGE
OF CAPITALISM

GEORGE M. YEAGER

© 2002 by George M. Yeager

This book was created by the editorial team at Literary Productions (www.literaryproductions.com).

This publication is designed to provide accurate and authoritative information in regard to the subject matter covered. It is sold with the understanding that the publisher and author are not engaged in rendering legal, accounting, or other professional service. If legal advice or other expert assistance is required, the services of a competent professional person should be sought.

> *. . . From the Declaration of Principles jointly adopted by a Committee of the American Bar Association and a Committee of Publishers and Associations.*

Although the information and data in this book was obtained from sources believed to be reliable, neither the authors nor publisher assume responsibility for its accuracy. Under no circumstances does the information in this book represent a recommendation to buy or sell stocks or funds.

Printed in the United States of America

10 9 8 7 6 5 4 3 2 1

ISBN 0-9717236-0-5

**MOONGATE
PUBLISHING**
New York, NY 10111

www.investingyournestegg.com

CONTENTS

INTRODUCTION

NO SENSIBLE DECISION CAN BE MADE . . . WITHOUT
TAKING INTO ACCOUNT NOT ONLY THE WORLD AS IT IS,
BUT THE WORLD AS IT WILL BE.

ISAAC ASIMOV

Andrew Carnegie once said, "Put all your good eggs in one basket and watch the basket." Although the philanthropic steel baron wasn't specifically talking about the stock market when he uttered this famous and often misquoted phrase, I can't think of better advice for today's investor. If he were an investment wizard, Carnegie might have instead counseled, "Buy a portfolio of several great companies, hold them for the long haul, and pay close attention to the names you own." It's a strategy I've followed throughout my 40-year career on Wall Street, and it has helped me to outperform the broad market. I want to help you do the same with your own nest egg, by giving you the advice you need to build a lasting and profitable portfolio that will serve you well for decades to come.

Before you begin this process, you must keep in mind that a great and awesome sea change has taken place around the globe.

We now live in a world without major wars between powerhouse nations. Economies everywhere are growing trade, thanks to international cooperation, extended prosperity, and dormant inflation. Plus, we enjoy a continued flow of scientific advancements. All the while, America, in particular, has strengthened its position as the world's number one superpower. The forces shaping these events are discernible, powerful, and, to a large extent, quantifiable.

We're experiencing a time of wealth expansion—both in degree and duration—without precedent in human history.

Those investors who understand what is happening are best positioned to capitalize on the future rewards. Despite recent weakness in the broad market, global economic unsettlement, and the strains of a war on terrorism, we are in a new leg of what has already been, for 20 years, the biggest and longest bull market in history.

This book will show you how to build your portfolio to benefit from this incredible environment by helping you to identify those stocks best positioned to prosper.

PATIENCE IS A VIRTUE

Having a good perspective of what lies ahead for the next several decades is a tremendous advantage for the long-term investor. After all, investing is a long-term sport. As legendary investor Warren Buffett has said, investing consists of "picking good stocks . . . and staying with them as long as they remain good companies." Sounds a little like Carnegie, doesn't it?

Yet it amazes me how few so-called investors follow what seems to be such incontrovertible advice. The majority of institutional and individual investors alike have become short-term obsessed, looking only for stocks with the best prospects for the next quarter or two. The average equity mutual fund manager turns over his or her portfolio at the rate of 90 percent annually.

This means almost every stock in the portfolio is bought and sold each year. And that's the *average*; many investors turn over their holdings two or three times a year, or more. In my vocabulary, these quick-change artists aren't investors. I call them "market participants," or even "speculators."

I realize it isn't easy to take a long-term view these days, even though that is the most profitable investment path to follow. The stock market has become a national pastime. We are constantly bombarded with news, alarms, appraisals, and advice from television commentators, newspapers, the Internet, and a myriad of magazines devoted to personal finance. These sources almost always recommend some kind of immediate action, leaving investors in constant anxiety about what changes they should make in their portfolios.

But when you get beyond the surface, you find that people are hungry for a stock strategy that is far different from the frenetic one followed by the rest of the crowd today. They want an approach that is sensible, long-term, and stable. They crave a portfolio of individual stocks or mutual funds that they can put away for only occasional review because they are confident their nest egg is invested in businesses with the highest probability of continued growth and profitability.

Institutions—such as pension funds, foundations, and endowments—have the same need. Their trustees are subject to similar Wall Street and media pressures, exacerbated by powerful consultants who advise diversification into an array of asset classes and constant rotation among them as valuations change. It's no wonder we have more than 10,000 mutual funds to choose from in today's market.

I have found, in almost four decades as a professional investor, that the good companies—those you can hold on to for a long time—share certain critical characteristics. This book will show you how to identify them. The truth is, even with all of the vast changes taking place in the world today, only a small percentage of companies are ideally positioned to thrive in this new era. They have the products, market dominance, global presence, technological infrastructure, and far-sighted and determined managerial culture to succeed.

In the pages that follow, you'll learn exactly how to find these companies. I'll begin by setting a context for the current investment environment, to demonstrate how the global economy has changed. I will then lay out the characteristics found in the limited number of companies most likely to prosper in the years ahead. Finally, I will profile 20 stocks I believe should be considered as part of every investor's core portfolio.

These aren't just good companies. They are *great* companies for the times we live in. They are the names you want to buy and keep. They are the stocks that should form the core of your nest egg.

CHAPTER ONE

THE GOLDEN AGE OF CAPITALISM

BECAUSE THE MEDIA LIVE ON BAD NEWS, WE GET BRAINWASHED
INTO THINKING WE'RE IN A PERIOD OF DIFFICULTY, WHEN WE'RE
LIVING IN THE MOST GLORIOUS PERIOD IN ALL WORLD HISTORY IN
ALMOST EVERY AREA YOU LOOK AT.

SIR JOHN TEMPLETON

The events and extraordinary changes that have taken place in just the last 10 to 15 years prove that the forces shaping our world are so irrepressible and positive in scope, we are justified in believing we have stepped into a period of global prosperity. I call it "The Golden Age of Capitalism."

Four vital developments explain why our universe has changed so radically. Though they are interrelated and mutually supportive—thus prolonging a virtual circle of salutary growth—each is of transforming importance.

THE TRIUMPH OF CAPITALISM

First on the list of events is the death of communism, along with the utter discrediting of the philosophy and fruits of socialism and all of its derivative manifestations. For more than 70 years—

indeed the heart of the twentieth century—the idea that state ownership, state planning, and state controls were essential to a functional economy was ascendant. That ascendancy is over. Those in communist economies earn wages that are far less than their freer neighbors. You may doubt that capitalism has embarked on a Golden Age, but you cannot deny its victory.

Socialism's surrender is manifest around the world through the privatization of nationalized industries and state-owned monopolies; slower growth in government spending and lower taxes are more commonplace. We're seeing an escape from the maze of regulations, and a dissolution of the kind of state capitalism that has predominated in Japan, South Korea, and much of the rest of Asia. In short, the *markets* are making global economic decisions, not the *politicians*.

The triumph of laissez faire is also a victory for political liberty. Governmental control over the way people make and spend their money usually goes hand in hand with the suppression of other freedoms. Never have so many people lived under democratic governments. China may remain schizophrenic in this regard, but freer choices in money matters are building tremendous pressure for broader liberties in that country as well. More to the point, we could never have a golden age of expanding global prosperity without having free enterprise virtually everywhere. This, in turn, spurs innovation, entrepreneurship, and competition. Centrally managed economies have finally learned this lesson.

A GLOBALIZED ECONOMY

We're seeing an economic interdependence of countries worldwide through the increasing volume and variety of cross-border transactions in goods and services. International capital flows are on the rise, and there is a more rapid and widespread diffusion of technology. Countries are freely trading goods and services, along with money, technology, data, and even factories and workers. They are able to do this without the impediment of sealed national boundaries, making the world's economies increasingly open, linked, and interdependent.

Free trade pacts have reduced tariffs, and world trade has boomed. Freely convertible currencies have facilitated this flow. A lifting of prohibitions and restrictions against foreign investment has flooded developing nations with needed capital. This global competition has helped to tame inflation, which is the bane of economic and business stability.

Globalization is another aspect of the markets' sovereignty over governments. The dimensions and momentum of this "one world of commerce" movement are unprecedented. The occasional efforts of some governments to abort or slow down the inevitable will prove counter-productive and eventually be abandoned. Globalization's ultimate promise is vigorous growth and a consequent rise in the wealth of nations.

AN EMERGING FIVE BILLION

The third great change in the world is the emergence of rapidly industrializing nations in what we not long ago called the Third World. We've seen it happen in Asia, Latin America, lagging areas of Europe, and some parts of Africa. Many of these countries were once colonies, expected only to supply raw materials to their motherlands. The standard of living among people in such places in 1950 wasn't much above the level it had been in 1850.

The economic consequences of vitalizing this portion of the globe, home to 80 percent of the total population, are enormous. There have been, and no doubt will be, sporadic setbacks. But the factories, technology, educated workers, entrepreneurial drive, and acquired marketing savvy are now in place. The clock will not be turned back. Living standards of ordinary workers have risen, and a vast new middle class has emerged. One pillar of the unfolding Golden Age is the creation of five billion potential customers for the world's goods and services.

REVOLUTIONARY TECHNOLOGY

Lastly, we have entered a post-industrial age: The Age of Information. Personal computers, modems, fiber optics, satellites, faxes, cellular phones, e-mail, and the Internet are gathering, processing, and communicating bits of information at ever-greater speeds and lower costs. This, in turn, is altering the fabric of life as dramatically as the steam engine, electricity, the automobile, and the airplane did generations before.

We can see the impact that the Information Age is already having on business efficiency and productivity, education, medicine, entertainment, and our everyday lives. Technological know-how has become a key determinant of wealth for both companies and entire countries.

We are only at the beginning of this innovative explosion. You've probably seen the startling statistics. Computing power doubles every 18 to 24 months (and the pace, as a result of recent breakthroughs in chip technology, promises to quicken). About 85 percent of all scientists who have ever lived are alive today. Half of all scientific research conducted in the United States took place within the last decade. Scientific knowledge is doubling every 13 to 15 years.

This technological revolution is closely linked to the other three revolutions. Communist governments could no longer prevent their citizens from finding out how much better people lived in free societies. Globalization would be a pale shadow of what it is today without computer networks and jet transport. Furthermore, the transfer of technology has allowed backwater nations to become competitive producers in rapid fashion.

THE FUTURE FORETOLD

These operative dynamics—a de-Communized world, globalization, vast new markets from emerging and newly liberated economies, and a technological revolution—are in place. There have been, and will continue to be, speed bumps in the evolution of these forces, such as a backlash against open markets, or an outcry for more governmental activism. But the factors shaping the future of world economies and societies are irreversible. There is no turning back from globalization.

Communism is discredited forever. All socialist programs are suspect. The developing nations will not relinquish their ambitions. Research labs are not going to close their doors.

In later chapters, we'll examine these transfiguring currents in more detail and examine the evidence suggesting the age we have entered not only belongs to capitalism, but will also vastly benefit from it. An investor who adopts the investment approach laid out in this book must be thoroughly convinced of this underlying premise. It is easy, as Sir John Templeton said, to read daily headlines about domestic and foreign problems and forget how far we have already come and how secure the changes are. Templeton and I are both convinced that my optimism about an expansive future is well warranted.

But this is an investment book, not a socio-political treatise. So, in the next chapter, we will discuss what all the aforementioned changes, which are likely to shape the world economic environment for at least the next quarter century, mean for investors.

THE RIGHT PLACE AT THE RIGHT TIME

How these extraordinary shifts in world dynamics should mold investment policy seems to be an elementary and critical question. Still, as far as I can tell, not many investors have asked it. Their attention is apparently focused elsewhere in today's nearsighted investment world.

Most market participants (I am reluctant to call them "investors") have become extremely short-term oriented. They are fixated on figuring out which sectors, industries, stocks, countries, or mutual funds are poised to be big winners over the next month, quarter, or year.

As long as investors are obsessed with short-term results, they don't care about the big picture. Their minds are too focused on today's headlines, analysts' latest quarterly profit projections, and year-to-date mutual fund rankings. Not only do they fail to see the forest, they even have trouble clearly seeing the trees. In other words, they can't tell the difference between a good company and a hot stock.

Granted, world and domestic events are constantly unfolding and you shouldn't ignore what's happening out there. But we've become so obsessed with daily developments, and often exaggerate their importance to such a degree that we lose sight of what investing is all about: buying good companies and staying with them as long as they continue to be such. This is the way great fortunes have been made. You profit by putting faith in enterprises that have shown, over many years, that they know how to cope with a volatile world and produce an ever-higher level of revenues and profits.

If this book does nothing more than make you rethink your approach to the market, your time horizon (the number of years you have to make your money work for you), and the fundamentals of investing and wealth accumulation, it will have accomplished much. Since the world scenario unfolding now will dominate the next couple of decades, investors should own the companies best positioned to profit from the events underway. Then you should hold on to them, not for weeks or months, but for years to come.

PRESENCE IS NOT ENOUGH

The challenge therefore becomes identifying these companies. That is the goal of this book: to relate macro developments to investment strategy, and to construct the dimensions of a core portfolio best suited for the early stages of our Golden Age.

Given developing events—an ever-growing and accessible population with the income to satisfy its hunger for the world's goods—the first investment operative that leaps to mind is that one must own companies with a global reach. You cannot make money from those upcoming billions of new customers if you are not there to sell them your goods and services.

But simply being multinational in operations is not enough to assure a company's success. In an environment where most companies, in almost any country, can make and sell goods just about anywhere, competitors abound. Companies will relentlessly look for ways to capture market share, including trying to undersell everyone else. To get or stay ahead, you must pare costs without sacrificing quality, market aggressively, retain good people in scattered outposts, and manage a complex far-flung operation.

In short, it's a tough world out there. The opportunities are immense, but the chance to make big money will always draw a horde of hungry contenders. Those who win will win big. But there will be more losers than winners. A select group will profit from globalization; others will be buried by it.

The best-positioned companies are those in such sound businesses they would survive even if globalization had never existed. They are well capitalized and well managed. They make products people want and are loyal to for years. And they have excellent prospects for sustaining superior growth.

In the search for better businesses, the basic principles of company analysis and investing predate any Golden Age thesis. Global reach, therefore, becomes the proverbial icing on an already-baked cake.

CHAPTER THREE

WHAT IS A "GOOD COMPANY"?

GROWTH STOCKS CAN BE DEFINED AS SHARES IN BUSINESS
ENTERPRISES WHICH HAVE DEMONSTRATED FAVORABLE UNDERLYING
LONG-TERM GROWTH IN EARNINGS AND WHICH, AFTER CAREFUL
RESEARCH STUDY, GIVE INDICATIONS OF CONTINUED SECULAR
GROWTH IN THE FUTURE.

T. ROWE PRICE (1939)

Why does anyone invest in stocks? Presumably it is to make his
or her money grow. If preservation of capital were the sole objec-
tive, a bank savings account would suffice. If income were the
primary goal, bonds would be a better choice.

By definition, then, it has always seemed to me that stock
investors should choose companies whose businesses, and profits, are growing.

I know there are other approaches to stock analysis, such
as concentrating on the assets of a company rather than its
earnings. In fact, we'll look at the most widely followed investment approaches, and compare and contrast their relative benefits, in Chapter Eleven. But if you want to be a long-term
investor, and find companies you can stick with, you must concentrate on those names with histories and current fundamentals

reasonable enough to give assurance they are consistent and reliable growth machines.

The average company's earnings grow about 6 to 7 percent a year. To qualify as a growth rather than an average company, a company's earnings must grow at least 10 percent a year. I look for companies doing even better, usually as high as 12 to 20 percent (or more).

Consistently rising profitability doesn't mean that a company won't occasionally have a flat or down quarter or two. This often reflects some necessary revamping to assure future growth. But for the investor with faith in a company's underlying strengths, the consequent dips in stock price—which can be severe in a market obsessed with short-term performance—are an opportunity to accumulate shares at an attractive discount.

PAST AS PROLOGUE

It's easy to identify companies with growth records, just as it's simple to pull up the names of mutual funds that have outperformed for the past three years. The challenge is deciding which companies can *sustain* this growth.

To make that judgment, one needs some history. There is a considerable difference between a proven growth company and an emerging growth company. A firm that has been in business for only a limited number of years has too short a record, not to mention too little experience dealing with difficult times and the strains of growth, to be able to project its future with any meaningful degree of certainty. Small emerging growth companies can be fabulous investments, but most disappoint and the risks are high. Therefore, well-established growth companies should form the core of most investors' portfolios. Those wishing to gamble on promising newcomers, and who have the stomach for the volatility that is a sure ingredient of such stocks, may then augment the core with a modest percentage of their nest egg.

Two elements are critical in a company's ability to sustain growth: pricing flexibility and recurring revenues.

PRICING FLEXIBILITY

The power to set prices at a level guaranteeing a healthy profit margin is near assurance that a company can generate the high return on equity necessary for continued expansion.

Pricing flexibility is hard to come by in the world I have painted. In the early stages of the Golden Age of Capitalism, the number of firms that will lose pricing flexibility will be greater than those that gain or enhance it. Low inflation, which has become a worldwide phenomenon, is the first reason. Oil, lumber, paper, and aluminum companies, for example, enjoy pricing flexibility only when commodity prices are on the rise. But no company, whatever its industry, can currently use inflation as an excuse for raising prices to improve profit margins. When Kellogg Company denied that reality and kept raising cereal prices, cheaper private labels began slicing away at its market share. The company is still scrambling to recapture its franchise.

In addition, globalization has meant the elimination of the protective barriers that allow companies to price their products and services without fear of the being undercut by the competition. Outside the United States, in particular, subsidies, tariffs, and other sheltering measures have fostered price levels that aren't sustainable in a fully competitive environment. Even in the United States, the deregulation of airlines, telephone companies, financial services, and utilities has introduced competitive pricing. When there is no protection, bloodbaths can ensue. That's a major reason behind so many mergers and consolidations in those industries, as companies scramble to consolidate their strengths and avoid internecine warfare. In Europe and Japan, too, protections are being lifted, starting in many cases with the same industries as in the United States.

The advent of the Internet has accelerated this process even further. I like to call the Internet "Darwinism on steroids." The Internet completely eliminates all global borders and allows just about anyone to compete with relative ease. We've already seen that good ideas are plentiful, and the competition so overwhelming, that only the fittest and fiercest competitors survive online. While such competition is a boon for consumers, it makes for a difficult operating environment for most companies.

In this new free-for-all environment, a company can command pricing flexibility only if it has a strong franchise—meaning a proprietary product, a brand name, a patent, and a presence—that allows it to *dominate* its market. In some instances, this franchise amounts to a near-monopoly of the market. The number one company in a market always has more options in its battle plan to maintain control.

Coca-Cola has its domestic soft drink competitors, but overseas it has many major markets practically to itself. The same is true of McDonald's in fast foods. Pharmaceutical houses with proprietary drugs obviously have a commanding advantage. Wal-Mart dominates discount retailing because it knows how to profitably deliver merchandise at rock-bottom prices. Gillette and Colgate-Palmolive rule their respective markets because of the revered reputation of their products.

All of these companies, it will be noted, sell directly to the final consumer. They are not middlemen. During these years of corporate cost-cutting crusades, companies are relentlessly squeezing suppliers. Any company whose revenues are a cost to someone else is in trouble. Wal-Mart can entice an ever-wider public with its discounts, but think about what that means to the many manufacturers it buys from. (When Sears, Roebuck was a young company, it succeeded with the same strategy—low prices made possible by pressure on suppliers.)

International Flavors and Fragrances once could be found in the portfolios of many growth stock managers. But this firm sells products to other companies, rather than to the public. For example, Colgate-Palmolive reduced its fragrances suppliers from more than two dozen to just a couple willing to lower prices in exchange for a big boost in volume. If kids want Mickey Mouse, they must come to Disney. If Disney wants Mickey Mouse caps, it can go anywhere in the world to cut a deal. Middlemen have no pricing flexibility.

RECURRING REVENUES

The second key determinant of a company's consistent ability to sustain growth is the degree to which its products generate repeat business. Repeat business comes from products that are consumed and need to be replaced, or from services that require repeating with regularity, perhaps on a contracted basis. Any company that starts every year with the knowledge it can count on getting the bulk of its revenues from the same customers it served the previous year, allowing it to at least match last year's sales figures, is obviously in a far better position than a company that has to start all over again. With an assured base, a company can concentrate on growth, by winning a larger market share, adding to its product line, or expanding geographically.

I believe this factor is so vital I won't invest in any company without reliable recurring revenues, even if that excludes numerous fast-growing names, such as technology manufacturers, which predominate many growth portfolios. Without the assurance of repeat revenues, a company reaches market saturation or risks technological obsolescence much more rapidly. Its rate of growth can also slow markedly in tougher economic times, with even sharper hits to its stock price. I didn't always employ this qualitative screen, and am perhaps the only investment manager who adheres to it without exception. I adopted this discipline after analysis of my past mistakes. I saw that the common denominator in more than 80 percent of my stock picks that went sour was the absence of recurring revenues.

Which products and services guarantee recurring revenues? We know that today's soft drink doesn't quench tomorrow's thirst, nor does today's stick of gum satisfy tomorrow's yen for a chew. Every new day brings the need for another shave and another blade. Indeed, pricing flexibility and recurring revenues are often complementary. It is because Coke, Wrigley, and Gillette have built such powerful brand names and customer loyalty that repeat business is all but assured.

Habits don't change overnight. People tend to use the same razors, toothbrushes, soaps, and drink the same sodas for many years, if not throughout their entire lives.

Wal-Mart has a different sort of expectation of a recurring revenue stream: loyal customers attracted by low prices maintained by inventory and distribution disciplines its rivals can't seem to match. In the service area, the best assurance of repeat business is a contract—such as State Street Corp.'s agreement with the mutual fund companies it handles back office and record keeping for, or Automatic Data Processing's contracts with the companies whose payrolls it runs.

The qualification of repeat business eliminates many companies from consideration in a portfolio of reliable growth companies, even those that sell fine products around the world. Any cyclical company is an example. DuPont is a blue chip company, but many of its products, and much of its profitability, are dependent on the business cycle. The same is true for Boeing. When the economy is sluggish and air traffic slows, it is easy to put off buying additional jets.

I avoid the makers of big-ticket items, which are usually purchases that can be postponed. General Motors and John Deere sell to the world, but few drivers replace their cars every year, and even fewer farmers regularly buy new tractors. I prefer those companies that make toothpaste and laundry soap, which are constantly consumed and replaced by millions of customers. These are also relatively low priced products, so even those in the emerging markets with low-level wages can afford them. And they won't be as affected by business cycles or crises. When the Southeast Asian economies fell into turmoil in 1997-98, infrastructure projects were cancelled and construction equipment manufacturers felt the impact. But men still had to shave, and everyone continued to shampoo their hair.

Technology *hardware* stocks don't make it through my repeat volume screen. Like Warren Buffett, I want to invest in "very predictable" businesses, those with fortunes that are foreseeable for the next 15 to 20 years. You know people are going to drink sodas and chew gum, but which technologies will be in demand a decade or two hence is pure guesswork. There is absolutely no assurance the dominance of these companies is sustainable. Technology companies are always vulnerable to some competitor's next breakthrough.

We've seen the consequence of this uncertainty in recent years. After many quarters of outsized growth and high expectations for the future, the stock prices of the vast majority of technology suppliers came crashing down beginning in 2000. Once Wall Street realized such growth was neither predictable nor sustainable, they sold off these shares in mass quantity, with many falling 70 to 90 percent or more in value.

That's one of the problems with technology companies. Most eventually become obsolete within a short period of time. Hardly any have recurring revenue streams. This doesn't mean they can't be great investments during the peak of their success. It's just that they aren't ideal "buy and hold" investments.

Take IBM and Xerox, for example. These were great growth stories from the late 1950s through the early 1970s. I owned large holdings in both companies during that time, as did many other institutional investors. With the recurring revenue streams that they possessed, they were earnings growth engines.

In the case of IBM, the company originally leased all of its computers. As a result, during each new fiscal year, IBM could count on receiving about 90 percent of the previous year's revenues, while adding new customers all the time. Then, once some Japanese competitors came in and started selling their equipment outright, IBM eventually had to follow suit. As the company's lease base became owners instead of renters, IBM's recurring revenue stream ceased, and it was no longer a growth stock. Shares of IBM struggled for many years, until new CEO Lou Gerstner took over in 1993 and began focusing on providing more outsourcing services—reintroducing a sizeable repeat revenue stream.

A similar turn happened with Xerox, which was one of the greatest growth stories of all time. Xerox once was the sole source of copy machines, which were available exclusively on a rental basis. Each time a copy was made, Xerox earned money. Once again, a Japanese competitor entered the market with a comparable machine that it offered for sale. Of course, Xerox had to follow suit, thus shutting off its successful recurring revenue stream.

I am convinced that there's far more money to be made from buying companies that successfully apply technology to their current line of business, as opposed to investing in technology companies directly. Indeed, you'll find that for most of the companies listed later in this book, the ability to adapt to technology is a key element in establishing a dominant position in their respective growth markets.

What's more, in addition to the prerequisite of pricing flexibility and recurring revenues, I look for companies with lots of customers. Colgate, Wrigley, and Gillette have millions of customers around the world in the *habit* of purchasing their products. There is no way the secular growth rates of such companies can deteriorate quickly. Of course, consumer preferences can and do change, but the attentive investor does not risk the rapid obsolescence inherent in a number of technology companies.

OTHER IMPORTANT NUMBERS

There is a corollary factor I consider to be critically important in choosing stocks. Companies with pricing flexibility and repeat revenues, enabling them to capture a high return on equity, also have the ability to maintain a high reinvestment rate. In formal terms, the reinvestment rate is the ratio of earnings retained in the business (net earnings less dividends paid out to shareholders), divided by a company's shareholder equity or net worth (total assets minus total liabilities). If a stock pays no dividend, return on equity and the reinvestment rate are the same.

Reinvestment and earnings growth rates tend to track each other closely. A consistent reinvestment rate of 15 percent is likely to result in average compound earnings-per-share growth of 15 percent, which is why many growth companies pay no dividends and instead plow all earnings back into the business. If the reinvestment rate is climbing, earnings should also rise.

It's widely recognized that the reinvestment rate is the best proxy for the rate at which a company can sustain its growth. I further consider the reinvestment rate to be a "proof statement" of that sustainability. It is a key component of my company evaluation process. Yet I rarely see the reinvestment rate offered in Wall Street analysts' reports, referred to in the media, or cited by professional managers.

ADDITIONAL CONTRIBUTORS TO GROWTH

Pricing flexibility—the proof statement of which is a high reinvestment rate—and repeat customers are essential to the definition of the kind of "good business" I want to invest in. You'll notice that I haven't mentioned price-to-earnings, price-to-book, price-to-sales, or other common valuation ratios. Such metrics are helpful in selecting stocks that are currently attractively priced, but they don't define a good business and will never serve as my primary selection screen. Furthermore, one should be wary of investing in a company with a balance sheet revealing its growth has been financed by piling on debt, instead of relying on the reinvestment of internally generated earnings.

Many professional investors assert that the most important element in assessing a company's future is the quality of its management. There is no doubt that these enormous geographically disperse global gorillas require managers with superior skills and long-term vision and discipline. Senior management is constantly faced with critical decisions, such as whether or not to spend millions to develop and market new products, or whether to pursue a strategic acquisition that can broaden the product line and provide entry into a new market.

Nevertheless, when companies build up an international franchise over decades, it would require an exceptionally incompetent management team to lose it. In addition, it takes consumers a long time to change their daily habits. Sam Walton built a magnificent retailing empire and Ray Kroc led McDonald's through years of extraordinary growth, but their deaths did not dampen the ambitions and progress of their companies. Successors can build on the foundations laid by genius. To cite Warren Buffett again, he once said he wants to own "businesses so good even a dummy can run them."

Incidentally, Buffett's rare mistakes—not just his many successes—confirm my beliefs. US Air, one investment Buffett later called a "mistake," unquestionably had recurring revenues. But it had little or no pricing flexibility. Salomon Brothers, another Buffett investment that ran into trouble, derived most of its revenues from high-risk transactions, rather than from, say, management fee income.

Companies grow by picking up market share, developing new products, buying other companies, and increasingly by expanding geographically. The ability to grow by global expansion is what can turn a good business into a potent perpetual money machine. Global reach is the other critical trait needed for sustained growth in the Golden Age of Capitalism.

Chapter Four

GLOBAL REACH: THE ADDED DIMENSION

THE SPREAD OF LIBERAL ECONOMIC IDEAS TO THE
THIRD WORLD HAS CREATED THE PRECONDITIONS FOR
A NEW GOLDEN AGE OF CAPITALISM.

DAVID B. HALE, CHIEF ECONOMIST, ZURICH GROUP

Five billion new customers!

That is fact, not hyperbole. There are hundreds of millions of potential consumers with rising incomes in places such as the Philippines, Chile, Turkey, and Poland. There are hundreds of millions more whose governments have finally opened their gates to foreign-made goods, such as China and India. In fact, in 2001 China joined the World Trade Organization. Others are coming around as well. Although Coca-Cola is now the leading soft drink maker in India, that country of nearly one billion once kicked out Coca-Cola for not revealing its syrup formula and giving up majority control of its local operation.

Elsewhere, Johnson & Johnson and Colgate-Palmolive have been selling products in Latin America for decades, but real profitability came only with the end of currency controls and discriminatory regulation—not to mention hyperinflation. Then there are the millions of people in countries that scuttled communism for free-market opportunities. Citizens in East Germany once only had cola from a state-owned bottler to quench their thirst, though the Coke name was quite familiar from television. Once the Berlin Wall was pulled down, Coke immediately invested more than $500 million and now dominates that thriving market.

Developed nations also promise expanded markets. The European Common Market has made it easy for an American company to make its wares in one European country and sell them freely throughout the rest of the continent, reducing costs and streamlining marketing. Japan, slowly and reluctantly, is increasingly accepting the inevitability of foreign competition on its shores.

But the leading companies from now on will be those selling to markets that are growing rather than maturing or declining. The prospects in these burgeoning markets are indeed awesome. There is a McDonald's for every 25,000 Americans, but only one for every 900,000 Asians. The average United States citizen drinks 310 eight-ounce servings of soft drinks in a year; 60 percent of the world's population live in markets where the average consumption is fewer than 10 servings annually.

THE FIRST ARE FOREMOST

The markets are beckoning, but which companies will ring up the sales?

We know they will be large companies. The task of exploiting dozens of distant markets takes enormous resources. Tambrands, for example, saw the global possibilities for its feminine hygiene products, but realized it couldn't exploit this potential on its own. It sold out to Procter & Gamble in 1997. Today women can buy Tambrands around the world. The controlling shareholders of battery maker Duracell judged that a higher

investment return would be realized by selling to Gillette, with all
of its manufacturing, financial, and marketing resources. In 1999,
Cadbury Schweppes sold the overseas rights for its soft drinks to
Coca-Cola, admitting that it couldn't expand internationally the
way it had hoped on its own.

Clearly companies with an infrastructure already in place
have a huge advantage. They have established beachheads from
which it is very difficult to dislodge. "Infrastructure" translates
into products and brands that have been advertised and promoted to near universal recognition, distribution systems that
may reach even remote villages, local facilities and possibly manufacturing plants, personnel who know the territories, all necessary permits and licenses, and strategic partners where needed.

"A multinational has operations in different countries," Al
Zeien, former chairman of Gillette, has noted. "A global company views the world as a single country." It sells the same products, uses the same production methods, follows the same corporate policies, and employs the same advertising. Good ideas
quickly infuse the entire system. Costs are spread over an ever-
widening base, creating economies of scale that translate into
higher profit margins. Competitive positions are constantly
strengthened, and attractiveness to investors grows.

It has taken decades and hundreds of millions of dollars to
erect these infrastructures, achieve brand name recognition, and
build the trust these companies now enjoy. Gillette and Coca-
Cola have been selling products to the world since early last century. McDonald's erected its first golden arches overseas in the
1960s. American International Group was actually founded in
Shanghai in 1919, and today is the dominant life insurer in China
and Southeast Asia.

Since foreign operations have tended to be more profitable
than domestic operations, the multinationals have plowed free
cash flow into their overseas operations, building quasi-monopo-
lies that are nearly impregnable. Late arrivals, attracted by a

latent global spending explosion, will face enormous outlays and frustrations. They may eventually turn into serious competition, but it will take years. Even a marketer with the ambition of Pepsi has largely ceded the underdeveloped world to Coke, as Burger King has to McDonald's. In the emerging markets, Procter & Gamble has lost its dominance in the oral care market to Colgate, which has a far stronger presence.

In recent years, those in the club are increasingly forming symbiotic ties to cement their hold on international markets. Johnson & Johnson and Merck have set up a joint venture in which the former markets Merck's drugs once they go off prescription. Staples offers Automatic Data Processing's payroll services to its small company customers. McDonald's signed a long-term contract with Disney, displacing Burger King in its parks. After all, why would Disney, with its global audience, continue to tie itself to Burger King, which has so little foreign exposure? McDonald's promotes Disney films, and Disney favors McDonald's for its theme park eateries. Coca-Cola is the sole provider of soft drinks to both Disney and McDonald's. When Coca-Cola's former chairman Robert Goizueta died in 1997, flags at McDonald's around the world flew at half-mast. Coke has helped McDonald's set up new operations abroad, since Coke operates in about twice as many countries as the hamburger giant.

These companies know they can reinforce each other's franchises. The same is true of mass-merchandiser Wal-Mart and the makers of leading brand name consumer goods. Who can rack up sales for them better than Wal-Mart? Woe to the second-raters in this new world. The rich will get richer.

The consumer-product multinationals have competitors to deal with in overseas markets, of course, including the local discount retailers and soft drink bottlers. These locals didn't have much competition until Wal-Mart and Coke arrived. Some have tried to stand their ground and take on their United States-based invaders. But they lack comparable resources to advertise and promote, as well as the glamour of the American products being flashed on television and movie screens. In most cases, these local companies suffer a slow death. Some see the handwriting on the console and sign up for a joint venture. In many cases, the owners simply sell out and retire under the palms.

There are exceptions. Not every American company can compete with local preferences. Anheuser-Busch, seeing hardly any growth in U.S. beer consumption, would like to go global in a big way. But beer drinkers are extremely loyal to local brands. Would a Dutchman give up his Heineken for a Bud? Anheuser would probably have to buy interests in local brewers, as it has in Mexico, to build sales abroad. Coffee drinkers, however, are open to experiment. Starbucks is even entering Italy, daring to bring American java into the land of cappuccino. Starbucks is also dipping heavily into tea-drinking Asia.

FAITH IN THE HOME TEAM

Thus far into the Golden Age, the companies best positioned to win in the global game are wearing American jerseys. Glaxo, Unilever, Allianz Worldwide, ABN-Amro, Cartier, and Carrefour Group are genuine multinationals with repeat-sale products and a strong global presence. Still, I prefer their U.S.-based rivals Pfizer, Colgate-Palmolive, American International Group, State Street Corp., Tiffany, and Wal-Mart. This is not narrow nationalism. I simply believe American companies have most of the advantages.

Those advantages will be examined in more detail in a moment. Needless to say, United States-based companies have already restructured and are in fighting trim. They are often the lowest-cost producers. They are not hampered by retrograde regulations, excessive social welfare programs, militant unions, or debilitating traditions and class structures. They operate in a country that is oriented toward profits, shareholders, and entrepreneurial initiative. They lead in important industries—among them software, fast foods, financial services, entertainment, and health care. And they sell to a world entranced with the American way of life.

It's true that there are some German and Japanese companies that dominate global markets and outshine their American counterparts. But these are capital equipment and durable goods manufacturers such as Siemens and Sony. The products made by these companies don't assure repeat revenues, and their rate of growth falls well behind our leading companies in business services and consumer goods.

I will always keep an eye out for strong foreign companies. But thus far into the Golden Age, the companies with the inside track, marketing know-how, widest brand recognition and acceptance, best supporting technology, and most impressive all-around muscle are American. Moreover, many U.S. companies—such as Automatic Data Processing, Disney, Gillette, Johnson & Johnson, McDonald's, Staples, Starbucks, and Wrigley—face *no* global competition of consequence.

In recent years, the U.S. dollar has been strong, prompting concern that American multinationals face a debilitating disadvantage. Their exports will be more expensive in foreign markets, critics claim, and currencies earned abroad will translate back into lower dollar profits.

I have not found the currency question to be a major problem. When appropriate and cost-effective, the multinationals know how to hedge this currency exposure through futures and forward markets. I'm not suggesting these companies aren't affected when a number of foreign currencies are devalued. But multinationals operate in a host of countries, which is a hedge in itself. Fluctuating currencies tend to at least partially offset one another. A company may lose against the Japanese yen and German mark, but gain against the Mexican peso and Canadian dollar. Since the second half of 1997, the U.S. dollar has risen strongly against most other currencies, but earnings gains for leading global companies have been moderated, not devastated.

Another ameliorating factor today is the importance of the manufacturing, assembling, warehousing, and distributions operations U.S.-based companies maintain abroad. By operating this way, labor, supplies, and many other costs are incurred in the local currency, with much of the earned money plowed back into the offshore facilities, rather than repatriated.

A strong dollar also brings some general blessings. American imports cost less, which further softens inflation's bite. And a strong dollar attracts foreign investment in U.S. stocks, especially in those companies with products that are familiar abroad.

In any event, currency fluctuations run in cycles, and their effect tends to be a wash over time. Whatever the climate, good companies somehow keep adding to their base of business.

CHAPTER FIVE

PREMIUM COMPANIES AT REASONABLE PRICES

STOCKS THAT ARE ABLE TO CONSISTENTLY MAINTAIN
EARNINGS GROWTH YEAR AFTER YEAR ARE OFTEN WORTH FAR MORE
THAN THE MULTIPLE WALL STREET CONSIDERS "REASONABLE."
GOOD GROWTH STOCKS, LIKE GOOD WINES, ARE OFTEN WORTH
THE PRICE YOU HAVE TO PAY.

PROFESSOR JEREMY SIEGEL, WHARTON SCHOOL

Even the best businesses can be doubtful investments if you have to pay too much for them. Price is never irrelevant, even when acquiring "priceless" old masters.

Indeed, you can't expect major corporations with expanding markets, weak or non-existent competition, pricing flexibility, recurrent revenues, and profits compounding at, say, 12 to 20 percent or more not to command a premium in the marketplace. That would be illogical. One expects to pay up for quality.

When you own companies with proven staying power, you don't have to worry about business cycles, or when to buy and sell. Even if the price-earnings multiple of a premier growth stock remained flat, your return could still be 12 to 20 percent a year, compounded, which beats the long-term performance of the Standard & Poor's 500 index by somewhere between 50 and 100 percent.

A stock's P/E multiple by itself (defined as its share price divided by earnings per share) tells us little. A high P/E, relative to that of the S&P 500, doesn't mean a stock is overpriced, any more than a relatively low P/E makes a stock a bargain. Every P/E has to be put into context with the earnings growth rate, for earnings are what ultimately determine stock prices. That's the only rational way to decide if a stock's price reflects business reality, or whether it has moved into the realm of pure expectation (as was true of most biotechnology companies in their infancy, or more recently with the Internet plays). A company with a P/E of 30 and earnings growth of 20 percent a year is a relative bargain compared to the S&P with a P/E of 20 and a growth rate of only 7 percent.

Viewed from the perspective of earnings growth rates and prices relative to that of the total market, the premiums on U.S. large-cap *sustainable* growth stocks are at the absolute *low* end of their historical relative valuation levels. You can even say that, from the vantage point of history, Figure 5.1 shows they are relative bargains.

FIGURE 5.1:
HISTORICAL VALUATIONS OF LARGE-CAP SUSTAINABLE GROWTH COMPANIES RELATIVE TO THE S&P 500

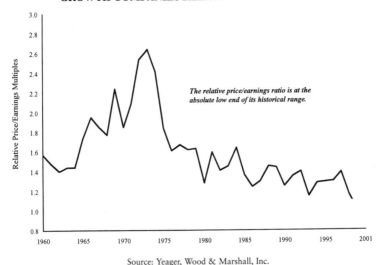

The relative price/earnings ratio is at the absolute low end of its historical range.

Source: Yeager, Wood & Marshall, Inc.

Please note that I am not saying "the market is undervalued; buy stocks." I am not a market timer, and I make no judgments about the market's overall value. I am simply saying that on a relative valuation basis, the earnings power of the best-positioned companies is not yet reflected in their prices.

The stocks of even the most proven and reliable companies fluctuate, although one could attempt to successfully time the acquisition of such stocks. In other words, you could try to buy on dips, when the market as a whole is weak, when sentiment has turned against a particular group, or when some event or analyst's comments send a stock down. In a market obsessed with short-term earnings momentum, measures taken by management to energize secular growth rates (such as stepped-up research and development investment and increased marketing expenditures) can penalize earnings for several quarters and cause sharp setbacks in stock prices.

A professional manager, with constant new cash flows, can take advantage of such opportunities. For individual investors, it may not be as easy. But if you have faith in a company, and its price premium is below its growth premium, it is always a safe time to buy. Too often those who wait for cheaper levels only watch the stock rise higher in price, as better-than-expected earnings come through, the stock gets new Wall Street sponsorship, or the whole market rises, bringing all P/Es along with it.

I'm not saying that if you have free cash you shouldn't take advantage of sell-offs of favored stocks, but you can outsmart yourself by trying to advantageously time either the market or individual issues. Sir John Templeton was once asked about when he thought it was a good time to buy stocks. "When you have the money," he replied. If you own a diversified portfolio, some of your stocks will have been acquired at the low end of their premium range, and some at the high end. If earnings keep growing, the acquisition price will not matter after a few years. These are stocks to *own*, not *trade*.

NOT SO NIFTY

My description of premier growth companies that deserve to be long-term holdings thus far will no doubt remind some readers of the early 1970s, when a group of big-name companies with a similar reputation were referred to as "one-decision" stocks.

The immediately preceding years in the late 1960s were wild times in the market; the "go-go era" of gunslingers who traded stories about new issues and small companies with hot prospects and then kited their prices ever higher, not unlike the micro-cap managers and momentum players of our day. The balloon burst in 1968, with a sharp market sell-off and an economic recession. Chastened investors decided they now wanted only big, respectable companies with earnings they could rely on, even through economic downturns. Banks and investment firms poured pension fund dollars into these issues. In a self-reinforcing process, good performance drew more assets into the stocks, and they were soon dubbed the "Nifty Fifty." When the 1973-74 crash came, these stocks plummeted. Some lost 80 percent of their value.

Am I leading investors up to the same primrose path, some 30 years later? I think not.

First of all, most of the Nifty Fifty may have been nifty for a time, but they weren't all great companies. Some still retain star status, including Coca-Cola, Gillette, Johnson & Johnson, Merck, Pfizer, and McDonald's. But what exactly were the near-monopolies of Avon Products, Polaroid, Digital Equipment, Revlon, or Burroughs? They were simply the story stocks of the time.

Secondly, the P/Es of the Nifty Fifty were, on average, more than three times their growth rates. Today, premiums accorded to the best growth companies are less than half of that. Some sported astronomical multiples of 60 and 70 times earnings. In the case of Polaroid, it was more than 90 times earnings. And premiums above the market's multiple were far higher, even though the companies that qualify as global powerhouses today (and I believe there are fewer than 50) are in a far better position to maintain and increase sales, since their market potential has expanded exponentially.

Long before the day my favorite stocks reach P/Es that are three times their underlying growth rates, I'll be out of them. But that day is still far away. To emphasize the point once again, I offer a strategy for the early stages of the Golden Age of Capitalism. The later stages will require a reassessment of tactics.

TWO-TIERED TOMORROW

I don't know if the premier growth stocks of our time will ever sell at the same multiples reached in 1972, but I am certain that the current modest multiples won't last forever. Growth stocks with a global reach will not stay this reasonable. The gap between their multiple and the market's multiple will widen. A marked two-tier market will inevitably evolve.

The reason is simple. As the Golden Age of Capitalism progresses, its contours and implications will become increasingly clear to more and more investors, as will the relatively small group of companies holding the winning hands. As some companies come through with ever-better numbers, while others fall behind, demand for those with proven power will escalate.

Investors will finally abandon their short-term strategies when they see the action is at a different table. Stock chasing, portfolio churning, and momentum mania, for all its frenetic intensity, won't pay off nearly as well as the stocks of a select number of companies able to conquer global markets. The old-fashioned notion of staying invested in businesses that sustain a high level of growth will come back into vogue, just as politicians eventually do the right thing after exhausting all other alternatives. As a result, the relative P/E ratios of these select few will move ever higher.

What is little recognized is how underinvested institutions are in these stocks, in contrast to the Nifty Fifty era. For example, mutual funds only own 7 percent of Coca-Cola, and the figure isn't much higher for many of the other companies we will examine soon. Pension funds, endowments, foundations, and mutual funds have been too absorbed in a myriad of other strategies—most of them short-term in nature—to focus on the bigger picture. In the 1980s, the emphasis was on buyouts and takeovers—asset plays rather than earnings. Concurrently, indexing became the craze, along with closet indexing by professional managers terrified of underperforming the benchmark by which they were judged. Only in the last few years, as their edge in the emerging Golden Age has started to gain recognition, have growth stocks come back into favor. But we are just at the beginning stretch of what we stated earlier will prove to be a powerful new upward run for global leaders. As that becomes evident, the institutions will be converted. They will then load up on these stocks, albeit at higher prices.

Foreign investors, who are currently underinvested in U.S. stocks, will likewise pile in. European investors have less than 20 percent of their assets in U.S. equities, a patently inadequate percentage given American leadership in the new global economy and the fact that U.S. equities constitute nearly half of the capitalization of the global equity market. Japan has hardly any money in U.S. stocks, but that, too, will change. Soon after currencies and markets started plummeting in Asia in the late 1990s, investors throughout the region started diversifying out of their own markets into U.S. stocks, which they had long disdained as too tame for tiger mentalities.

Another important trend abroad is the conversion to pay-as-you-go pension systems to fund the plans. Some portion of those accumulating assets will certainly be allocated to equities, including foreign equities. And overseas investors in the U.S. market, whether institutions or individuals, will buy the names long familiar to them: Coca-Cola, McDonald's, Colgate, Disney, Gillette, and Wrigley.

A number of domestic trends will also buttress the demand for these stocks. We're seeing signs of a slowdown in the U.S. after a period of unprecedented growth. Companies with earnings that continue to advance in spite of economic weakness are especially treasured in times like this. When interest rates are low, as they are now, stock multiples rise. Growth stocks, in particular, benefit from this trend. A steadily rising future stream of earnings and dividends becomes increasingly valuable, particularly when compared to bonds with falling yields. Of course, you want to find companies that have managed their businesses so well that you have a high degree of certainty about the continuation of those future earnings.

Finally, the present demographics are favorable to growth stocks. We know how many billions of dollars have poured into mutual funds over the past few years as the baby boomers—76 million strong—have become serious about saving for retirement. Americans between the ages of 34 and 44 save only 7 percent of their income, but from 45 to 54, the figure leaps to 23 percent. The oldest boomers have just entered their fifties; the youngest are still in their thirties. As investors, they will pour trillions of dollars into equities for another 10 to 15 years. These huge capital inflows are already building up demand for stock that exceeds the supply of superior businesses.

A well-defined two-tier market is therefore all but inevitable. Several ingredients have yet to kick in, most notably a lengthening of investor time horizons. But they will come. And there is nothing wrong with a two-tier market. It is the normal state of affairs. If one group of stocks is manifestly superior to the others, in terms of sustainable earnings growth, it should be accorded premium status. It is the current situation that is abnormal, even extraordinary. There is little correlation now between P/E multiples of companies and their sustainable growth rates. Stocks with low business risk are available at low prices.

Take advantage of this anomaly. The time may well come when these stocks, even with their superior growth rates, will indeed be too expensive. However, those who buy now will benefit not only from double-digit earnings growth, but also from a likely expansion in the multiple of those earnings. The rewards will be high for years to come.

CHAPTER SIX

THE PAST AS PRECEDENT

HISTORY DOESN'T REPEAT ITSELF, BUT IT RHYMES.

MARK TWAIN

Talk of "new eras," like the Golden Age of Capitalism, is always suspect. That's why I want to more closely examine the basis of my faith about the future.

We know that long periods of extraordinary economic growth and spreading affluence, with capitalism as the ignition source, are possible. Why? Because they have happened in the past. As a matter of fact, historians have labeled other periods as Golden Ages, though I believe their glitter will pale in comparison with the possibilities of the decades now before us.

WHAT SCIENCE WROUGHT

The most extensive and impressive past display of capitalism's bounty was spawned by the Industrial Revolution. It would not be an exaggeration to say that before then, the vast majority of people in the world lived at about the same level of comfort as they did in the Middle Ages. When machine production arrived, it created an abundance the world had never seen before.

Though James Watt patented his first steam engine in 1769, making it possible to supersede men and horses as sources of power, and thus firing the first shot in the revolution, it took decades to convert an age-old agrarian, handicraft system into a machine-manufacture economy. The railroad, steamship, and telegraph appeared in the first half of the nineteenth century, but it was in the second half that the pieces came together and the industrialization process gathered momentum. The introduction of the Bessemer process of making steel in 1856 was a major catalyst in creating a revived economy built on the forged metal. The new conversion process drastically lowered the cost of steel. Then, in the 1870s, came the telephone, the dynamo that could convert mechanical energy into electrical energy, along with the light bulb. The internal-combustion engine and radio were invented before the end of the century, and the flight of Kitty Hawk was not far behind. In the 70 years between 1790 and 1860, the United States Patent Office granted a total of 31,000 patents; in the 70 years from 1860 to 1930 it granted 1.5 million.

FUNDING A REVOLUTION

The enterprises needed to turn patents into products were far larger and more expensive than any known before. Major capital was required. That called for a pooling of the resources of a multitude of investors, rather than reliance on the wealth of a single person or a partnership. It called for a corporate structure that would give investors liquidity and freedom from the companies' liabilities, particularly since those companies were increasingly run by hired managers rather than hands-on owners. The infrastructure for liquidity was in place: Joint-stock companies, or corporations, had existed for a very long time. The London Stock

Exchange was chartered in 1698 and the New York Stock Exchange was launched in 1817. But those who bought stock risked losing all of their property, even if they had made a small investment in a large company, because shareholders assumed full liability for the company's actions. Limited liability companies that restricted an investor's financial exposure to the amount he or she had committed were first authorized in England in 1856, and soon after in the United States, France, Germany, and elsewhere.

Increasingly, corporate structures took dominance over proprietorships and partnerships. By 1900, 70 percent of industrial labor in the United States worked for corporations, and by the end of World War I, the number reached nearly 90 percent. The volume of trading on the floor of the New York Stock Exchange passed the 100 million share mark in 1900. The following year saw J.P. Morgan's formation of the United States Steel Corporation, the prototype of modern financial capitalism. As Robert Heilbroner and Aaron Singer note in *The Economic Transformation of America*, the corporation "was a social invention every bit as powerful as the technical inventions it controlled."

A LIMITED CORNUCOPIA

The era from the 1860s to the 1910s is similar to the one we are now entering in important ways far beyond the fruition of revolutionary technology. Britain's hegemony in Europe—and indeed, through her vast empire, in much of the world—assured no major challenge to peace. Until Britain's naval rivalry with Germany began, no "cold war" equivalent drained off capital. Prices were stable for many years, and as new innovations introduced new efficiencies, they actually declined. Ever since the repeal of Britain's Corn Laws in 1846 (which permitted the duty-free import of foreign wheat only if it reached certain high prices), the principle of free trade had been triumphant. Capital, too, flowed across borders without hindrance. It was largely British money, for example, that financed the American railroads. Labor was mobile as well, even more so than today, since immigration was largely unrestricted. In the quarter century before the outbreak of war, some 15 million people came to the United States to live.

Not long into the new century, trade protectionism and immigration barriers began to appear as national rivalries intensified. But, on the whole, the period from 1860 to 1911 was indeed a time of extraordinary openness, growth, and progress. By the end of that period, prior to the assassination of Archduke Ferdinand in Sarajevo that sparked World War I, world gross domestic product was rising at an average annual rate of 2.1 percent. That may not seem startling today, but it was double the rate of the preceding century. The United States did far better. From the end of the Civil War to the outbreak of World War I, GDP expanded at an annual rate of about 4½ percent, which translated into an 18-fold increase in the output of manufactured goods. This wealth creation provided the capital to generate more wealth.

The rising tide lifted standards of living wherever industrialization took place. In Great Britain, about 85 percent of the population was living at or near the poverty line at the advent of the nineteenth century. By its end, the number dropped to less than one-third. You can imagine what the arrival of electricity in homes, the convenience of subways, the affordable ($500) Model T that Henry Ford started mass-producing in 1913, the cheap entertainment of the radio, phonograph and motion pictures, and the advances in medicine and public hygiene must have meant to the comfort and well-being of millions of people. Nor had there ever been such a degree of economic and social mobility, where people could take entrepreneurial risks and rise into the middle class or even into the upper echelons of the truly wealthy.

It's no wonder this period has often been called a Golden Age. (Mark Twain, in a book co-authored with Charles Dudley

Warner, decided "Gilded Age" was more appropriate, considering the conspicuous materialism of the time.)

But the largesse had its limits.

Most importantly, the gifts of industrialization were confined to a few nations. A majority of the world's population shared in little of the new wealth. In those countries that thrived, the disparities in lifestyle between the wealthy and the masses in overcrowded cities were immense. Although many still deplore the gap dividing rich and poor in both developed and developing nations today, 100 years ago there was no income tax to trim the lifestyles of the fortunate and pay for the amelioration of the poor through government services.

There were continuous sharp swings in prosperity and deep recessions. During the slump of 1873, the New York Stock Exchange had to shut down for 10 days to stem a bleeding market. The depression of 1893 was the most severe in U.S. history, except for the 1930s. True, the Federal Reserve System, created in 1913, did little to prevent the Great Depression of the 1930s and, in fact, probably contributed to its advent. But in recent years, it and other central banks have been far more understanding and skilled in mitigating the severity of business cycles. From 1890 to 1945, the U.S. economy contracted 5 percent on three occasions, 10 percent twice, and nearly 15 percent a couple of additional times. Since 1945, the most severe decline in output occurred in 1987, and it only dropped 3 percent.

No restraints were in place to moderate capitalism's early excesses. Market chicanery of every sort flourished. The Securities and Exchange Commission wasn't born until the 1930s. The rules and regulations, and mechanisms for the enforcement of those rules and the settlement of disputes over their interpretation, are essential to investor confidence and a healthy securities market. The nascent exchanges in developing economies are rapidly adopting those that have evolved in New York and London.

Another critical difference between that earlier era and our own is the existence of today's jet transports and global telecommunications systems. It was impossible then to have a linked one-world economy in the same sense that we have today. We are now, in effect, all neighbors rather than distant trading partners.

I believe the period from 1860 through the first decade of the twentieth century will pale in comparison to the unprecedented dynamics of the present era. As a result, I prefer to call that earlier time a "Silver Age," because it pales next to this new Golden Age.

Chapter Seven

A Century of Capitalism on the Defensive

THE FUNCTION OF SOCIALISM IS TO RAISE SUFFERING
TO A HIGHER LEVEL.

Norman Mailer

World War I tarnished the Silver Age. In wartime, bullets replace goods as the commodity of exchange. Borders are sealed and barricaded. Governments appoint committees to centrally control the allocation of economic resources. Free markets give way to agency directives, procurement bureaucrats, rationing, heaving taxation, and price controls. And once the cannons are stilled, pre-war norms are never wholly restored.

At the war's end in 1918, vindictive and mistrustful nations abandoned the open competitiveness that had been building a more prosperous world, and shrank back into self-protective isolationism. The United States spurned the League of Nations. In 1930 came the Smoot-Hawley Tariff, which erected the highest trade barrier rates in history. Canada, Britain, and other countries retaliated. As would be expected when tariff walls were being raised everywhere, world trade plummeted. The level of exports as a percentage of world production reached in 1913 wasn't surpassed until 1970. Capital flows, too, dried up as a consequence of other nationalist restrictions.

World War I also witnessed the birth of communism in Russia, along with the propaganda for state ownership it relentlessly exported. If there had been a chance for democratic capitalism to prevail everywhere else, the inflation in Germany of the 1920s and the world depression of the 1930s doomed it. Both Fascist Italy and Nazi Germany pursued a policy of "autarky," or self-sufficiency, which meant high tariffs and import quotas. Both countries subordinated business and labor to the higher needs of the fatherland and its armies.

Even where political democracy prevailed—and it became a scarce commodity—governments were expected to shepherd economic systems enfeebled by the Great Depression. These paternalistic approaches were sometimes called "state capitalism." America's New Deal was one variety, with its federal employment for public works projects, the passage of a host of welfare measures, and the creation of a plethora of regulatory agencies. In 1929 total government expenditures in the U.S.—federal, state, and local—added up to less than 10 percent of gross national product. By the 1970s, it had reached one-third.

SOCIALISM ASCENDANT

Post-war memories of the Depression dictated economic thinking. It was almost unanimously accepted that unfettered capitalism led to boom-and-bust cycles and intolerable levels of unemployment (which had reached nearly 25 percent in the U.S. in the 1930s). For almost the next 50 years, the belief prevailed—even in the non-communist world—that some degree of government control, from surveillance and planning to outright ownership of key industries, was necessary for economic well-being and full employment. Capitalism was on the defensive.

It's becoming easy to forget how thoroughly the idea of government paternalism dominated most of the twentieth century. At its height, communism reigned in 23 countries. India, with one-sixth of the world's population, to a large degree emulated the Soviet economic model, with five-year plans, state ownership of major industries, and endless regulations, quotas, permits, and licenses. In most of Asia and South America, too, the state as puppeteer prevailed.

In Britain, just two months after Germany surrendered, Churchill was voted out of office in favor of the Labour Party and its socialist agenda. Railroads, ground transport, shipbuilding, coal mines, iron and steel, docks and harbors, telecommunications, oil exploration and production, electrical power, and much of car manufacturing were quickly nationalized. In France, the government took over banking, electricity, gas, coal, and other industries. In Germany, the government owned at least 25 percent of the shares of about 650 companies. Along with the nationalization of key industries came confiscatory taxes on businesses and individuals, cradle-to-grave social welfare programs, unrelenting pro-labor legislation, and a skein of regulatory agencies to spew out endless red tape.

Though "socialism" was anathema to most in the U.S. as a blood relative of communism, the government grew relentlessly as regulator, employer, and spender of the national wealth.

For 70 years the world was dominated by the idea that state authority over the economy was essential for the well-being of society—whether expressed as Russian and Maoist communism or the benign socialism of the democracies. It is only when you consider how this notion that "Big Brother knows best" prevailed that you can appreciate what a remarkable turnaround has taken place at the dawn of this new century.

POCKETS OF PLENTY

Not that there weren't periods when most countries in the free world enjoyed prosperity in spite of the shackles of social democracy. In the 1950s and 1960s, a pent-up demand in the wake of depression and war assured a robust global economy. From 1950 to the oil shock year of 1973, world economic growth averaged a remarkable 4.9 percent.

For the United States, which emerged from the war as the only real power in an impoverished and exhausted world, it was an exuberant time. Some quarters saw the economy growing at a 9 percent annualized rate. Productivity, on average, rose nearly 3 percent a year. Inflation was practically nil. In some years, prices even fell. Unemployment ran under 5 percent most of that time. Incomes rose steadily, so that standards of living improved even though, in those days, households usually had only one bread-winner. And the Dow Jones Industrial Average, at 200 in 1950, hit a high of 985 in 1968. Some have called the quarter century cul-minating in the oil crisis of the mid-1970s another Golden Age.

Much of the the country's post-war prosperity, however, was fueled by government spending. In the 1950s money was poured into the G.I. Bill to provide educational financial support to vet-erans, along with the Federal Aid Highway Act that created the crux of our highway system. In the 1960s came the Great Society programs and the Vietnam War, major causes of the inflation soon to follow and a bear market that lasted from 1973 to 1982. Today, the national consensus appears to be tilting towards restraint in government spending, to which both political parties profess to subscribe.

The Vietnam War was terrible evidence that the Cold War still raged, and that the menace of communism required constant vigilance and struggle. Socialism and/or dictatorships reigned in much of the world.

Nor had the then Third World come far in its bootstrap efforts or opened up the markets that exist today. With hind-sight, this has been recognized by many world observers. "The U.S. is seeing business opportunities today that absolutely dwarf anything that existed in our supposed Golden Age of the

1950s and 1960s," wrote Edward Yardeni, chief economist of Deutsche Morgan Grenfell.

American companies are far better managed and more competitive today than they were in the 1960s. The economy's output per capita is also on the rise, as is the average American family's income.

The 1950s and 1960s were extraordinary, if flawed, years for the United States. They offered another example of the capacity we have for dynamic growth. But we needn't indulge in nostalgia, for we are in an era that will be even more rewarding.

CHAPTER EIGHT

AN ECONOMY WITHOUT BORDERS

THE IMPORTANT TRENDS OF THE AGE TRANSCEND NATIONAL
BOUNDARIES AND NATIONAL SOVEREIGNTY.

ROBERT BARTLEY, EDITOR, *THE WALL STREET JOURNAL*

Globalization is new under the sun because its dimensions are unprecedented.

Of course, trade among nations has existed as long as nations themselves. The period before World War I was one of expansive world trade unimpeded by barriers to the mobility of goods or capital. But 100 years ago there were no jet planes and computer networks to effect, at insignificant cost, instantaneous transfers of money and overnight shipments of goods. Investors supported enterprises outside their countries' borders, but companies could not have plants in multiple countries. Nor was there truly a global economy, since most countries were mere colonial suppliers of raw materials to the industrialized elite.

As World War II drew to a close, nations were determined not to repeat the isolationist follies that followed World War I. Two years after the war's end, 57 nations agreed to set up an

International Trade Organization, which led to the General Agreement on Tariffs and Trade, now succeeded by the World Trade Organization. Regional trading blocs based on reciprocal lowering of tariff barriers have flourished, including Europe's Organization for Economic Cooperation and Development (OECD); the North American Free Trade Agreement (NAFTA); the Mercado Cono Sur (MERCOSUR) arrangement among Argentina, Brazil, Chile, Bolivia, Paraguay and Uruguay; and the Association of Southeastern Asian Nations (ASEAN).

U.S., European, and Japanese multinationals now have factories, retail outlets, distribution networks, research centers, and other facilities all over the world. Indeed, if governments initiated globalization, it is now being driven largely by corporate entities. One half of the world's imports and exports are accounted for by transactions between companies and their foreign affiliates (or parents), and half of all products manufactured in the United States now have one or more components made in another country. In-demand professionals and managers can be hired anywhere, especially since English has become the universal language of our time.

More and more, companies, financial institutions, and investors are operating as though national boundaries are irrelevant lines on a map. In *World Class: Thriving Locally in the Global Economy*, Harvard Business School professor Rosabeth Moss Kanter points to the Mazda Miata, a car designed in California and financed in New York and Tokyo, whose prototype was built in Worthing, England, and which was assembled in Michigan and Mexico, using electronic components invented in New Jersey and fabricated in Japan.

Cross-border mergers and acquisitions, in such industries as drugs, finance, tires, publishing, food, engineering, and communications, have become commonplace. There's no doubt they will continue. The opinion expressed by Thomas Middlehoff, chairman of Germany's Bertelsmann publishing house, will no doubt prevail: "There are no German and American companies. There are only successful and unsuccessful companies."

TO WIN, YOU HAVE TO PLAY

Why did governments convert to open-door policies, abandoning the often extensive measures they designed to protect their important industries, discourage imports and promote exports, and keep a firm hand over capital flows? They had little choice.

If you want to participate in booming world trade, you can't shut yourself up behind locked doors. You must allow your currency to be readily converted into those of your trading partners. If you want foreign capital to help build your phone lines, power plants, and air and sea ports, you cannot subject overseas companies to endless harassment. You know that companies are the chief transfer agents of technologies and managerial skills. And you know that partnerships with multinationals can open up world markets to your domestic manufacturers.

The welcome accorded to foreign investors and competitors coincided with the removal of obstructions to internal competition, as a free-market mindset replaced the belief in central planning. Governments could see, in today's global arena, that the more attractive they made their economic environment, the more likely they were to win "beauty contests" for outside capital that could stimulate growth, productivity, and employment. A country with sound monetary policies, a balanced budget, control over inflation, no stifling labor regulations, and a determination to privatize state-owned industries and deregulate others will be the favored recipient of stimulative new investment and won't have to pay a risk premium when it borrows from the capital markets.

Currency traders and institutions such as pension funds, mutual funds, and hedge funds have become the "vigilantes" of world markets, moving billions around in ways that are more effective in restraining government excesses than even the monetary might of central banks. Their power to judge governmental policies and decide to buy one country's bonds rather than another's has eroded national sovereignty.

Moreover, the evidence has piled up showing that it is worth taking the risks of letting the outside world in. Instead of declining standards of living, as was feared when protections were dropped, the standard of living has risen. Studies show that open economies grow far faster than closed ones. Economist and author Adam Smith's principles have been applied to a global economy, because the invisible hand is more effective than the bureaucrat's.

Everything happens faster today. Still, it took decades for globalization to become a meaningful reality. Governments needed time to be convinced of the benefits of openness. Infrastructures and a critical mass were needed before the new technologies could become a binding force. After all, computer and telecommunications networks mean little until the machines and skilled operators are spread universally and interconnected. The inflation of the 1970s had to be conquered to provide the stability that would give businesses confidence to expand abroad. Nor could globalization have been possible while the Cold War still divided a nervous world.

Now that the foundations are in place, globalization will proceed at a much faster pace. The world will, in essence, become one market, with the same brands sold in similar malls and arcades everywhere. There will be transition hardships, but the penalties for insularity and the rewards of openness are too enormous to deny.

Chapter Nine

THE TECHNOLOGICAL REVOLUTION

THE GLOBAL NATURE OF THE DIGITAL WORLD WILL INCREASINGLY
ERODE FORMER AND SMALLER DEMARCATIONS. SOME PEOPLE FIND
THIS THREATENING. I FIND IT EXHILARATING.

NICHOLAS NEGROPONTE

How can something as nebulous as "information" be as seismic in impact as the railroad, the electric light, the automobile, and the airplane?

The answer is all around us. The computer's ability to gather, store, analyze and respond to data, and telecommunications' ability to transmit it instantaneously to the world, are revolutionizing economies and lifestyles. Nearly half of U.S. households now have computers. Cellular phones are as ubiquitous as umbrellas. Those unseen information genies called microprocessors command our microwave ovens, refrigerators, TV sets, and cars.

The implications for business, and therefore economies, that these advanced technologies have brought are extremely consequential in stimulating non-inflationary growth. Without computers, FedEx says it would need to generate two billion pieces of paper annually and employ 20,000 people to handle them. Wal-Mart's success has rested importantly on its ability to minutely and instantly track and analyze sales, inventories, and shipments. Computers have become such an integral part of almost every enterprise today, whether in the private or public sector, that *Forbes* has commented, "Were they all suddenly to stop working, western civilization would collapse."

Much of the downsizing we've seen in American industry, middle management, and factories over the past decade has been possible precisely because of technology-driven efficiencies. One out of two workers in the U.S. is now likely to use a computer. When companies can generate the same output with fewer workers, they become more competitive, productive and profitable, while holding the line on prices.

In the late 1990s, the United States spent close to $500 billion a year on information technology, with high tech accounting for some 40 percent of real growth in the country. And this was non-inflationary growth, just as technological changes a century earlier brought down prices then. The costly personal computer of 1981 could do 330,000 instructions per second. Today's $1,000 computer can do more than 200 million. A three-minute phone call from New York to London cost around $8 in 1976. Today that call can be made for less than 20 cents. As Stephen Shepard, *Business Week's* editor-in-chief, has written, information technology "boosts productivity, reduces costs, cuts inventories, facilitates electronic commerce. It is, in short, a transcendent technology—like railroads in the nineteenth century and automobiles in the twentieth."

Economists have been pointing out for some time that we are now in a post-industrial society. In 1900, 39 percent of the American labor force worked in agriculture. Today it's a mere 3 percent. We still produce surpluses. For decades now, a reverse trend has been evolving. This time workers are leaving factories rather than farms. In the mid-1960s, the number of those working in manufacturing peaked at 28 percent. Today it's 16 percent.

Though the percentage is higher in Europe and Japan, it's not substantially so and is on the decline. Services—health care, financial services, retailing, restaurants, entertainment, and travel—are now the preeminent employers.

The post-industrial Information Age has changed the balance of power in the world. Knowledge and know-how have become more important in creating wealth than land, resources, labor, or even capital. The country whose enterprises are technologically enabled to produce goods more efficiently and cheaply that can be effectively marketed worldwide will reap the benefits of increased exports, a humming economy, and full employment at higher wage levels. Today's superpowers are those with economic muscle, not armies. How else could little Hong Kong or Singapore, without territory, a large population, or natural resources achieve such success?

The Information Age is still young. It was born with the invention of silicon microchips in 1970 and the introduction of the personal computer in 1982, but it took some evolutionary years to make computers widely affordable. We are now only at the threshold of their full promise, especially since their capabilities keep increasing while their costs decline. Parallel advances are taking place in communications, and the possibilities of the Internet have barely been scratched.

Investors can, of course, make bets on the companies that come up with the latest advances. But technology has always been a difficult investment sector. If you get it right, or lucky, the rewards are huge. But, routinely, some fresh innovation quickly torpedoes a company's advantage. Eleven new companies are created every week in the Silicon Valley alone. The field is always shifting and treacherous. The reasons touch back to the general absence among technology companies of the two prerequisites for *sustainable* growth that I insist on: pricing flexibility and repeat revenues. Dominant leadership rarely endures beyond even one technological product cycle because of rapid innovation by new competitors—and hence early obsolescence. Moreover, technology products—unlike toothpaste—are not normally consumed, and their replacement can be postponed.

I prefer to invest in those companies best positioned to exploit the latest technology and thereby dominate their markets. When *Forbes ASAP* named "America's Best Technology Users" a few years ago, the short list included some of my favorite names: Disney, Wal-Mart, Home Depot, Marriott International, Starbucks, and McDonald's. These enterprises, viewed as low-tech by some, offer a safer way to cash in on the future of technology.

Chapter Ten

America the Bountiful

THE MAN WHO IS A BEAR ON THE FUTURE OF THE UNITED STATES
WILL GO BROKE.

J.P. Morgan

When the decade of the 1990s began, it was widely believed that the United States was well on its way to becoming a second-rate power.

The critics were ruthless. They claimed we were a crime-ridden, pollution-prone, drifting, demoralized country. Our federal deficit was out of control. Our corporations were run by mere caretakers, passive and complacent, incapable of formulating long-term strategies. We had lost our work ethic. Against the assiduous, low-paid, rising toilers of the Third World, our workers would soon slide from the middle into the poverty class. A nation of self-indulgent consumers, we saved so little of our earnings that we would run out of capital to stoke further growth. Our widening trade deficit showed we had lost the ability to make goods the world wanted to buy. We couldn't seem to produce an automobile that could compete in quality with those made in Japan or Germany.

America was also lagging in high-tech. Our world share in the production of semiconductors fell from 60 percent to 40 percent, and though we still had the lead in computers, it was feared that Japan was about to seize it from us, as it had done with consumer electronics. The video, radio, and hi-fi equipment in our homes was labeled Sony, Panasonic, Hitachi, and Aiwa. There were no U.S. makers of VCRs or CD players.

No wonder the 1990 World Competitiveness Report ranked the United States twelfth (out of the 23 industrialized countries surveyed) in product quality, tenth in on-time delivery, eleventh in training workers, and second to last in planning for the future. Japan was first in every one of those categories, and Germany rated either second or third. In his first election campaign in 1992, Bill Clinton frequently cited those two adversaries as symbols of the challenges we faced as a nation. Books were written extolling the "Asian Model," such as Clyde Prestowitz's popular *Trading Places: How We Allowed Japan to Take the Lead.* Japanese companies and entrepreneurs, flush with success, were buying up America, from golf courses to Rockefeller Center. No doubt about it, Japan was well on its way to replacing the United States as the world's number one economy. The U.S. had fallen out of the running. Even Europe was viewed as being more superior.

AMAZING REBOUND

What a miraculous difference a very few years can make! In every World Competitiveness Report since 1993, the once limping United States has ranked first overall. This growth was achieved with inflation at its lowest level in 30 years. At the same time, Japan has been struggling with recession and self-doubt. Britain has emulated U.S. policies and is doing well, but continental Europe has been mired in slow growth and double-digit unemployment.

Globalization explains much of this success. The United States is the world's largest exporter. We sell both sophisticated capital goods and everyday consumer staples. Services are escalating in importance. Although we've seen a drop in overall capital spending, the fastest-growing segment remains technology, which can only continue to balloon in response to the world's hunger for computers, software, and telecommunications in the Information Age. America has a well-established lead in most knowledge industries, including the Internet.

True, the monthly trade reports still show that we import more than we export. But these numbers need examination. The trade deficit is larger in absolute terms than it was a decade ago. However, thanks to our expanding economy, it's considerably lower as a percentage of our gross domestic product. In addition, nearly 40 percent of U.S. imports originate from foreign affiliates of American companies. They represent intra-company transactions, reflecting the multinationals' decisions to make labor-intensive, low-value-added items abroad. At the same time, U.S. industry now earns more than three times as much from goods made, assembled, and sold overseas by foreign affiliates than it does from the exports of goods originating from domestic plants. Those sales are not counted as "exports" shipped from our shores. One prominent economist noted that when those sales are calculated, the trade deficit actually turns into a hefty *surplus*.

A HOUSE IN ORDER

The collapse of the Soviet empire left the United States as the only truly global power. Militarily, no other country can seriously compete with our stealth aircraft, cruise missiles, laser-guided bombs, and satellite surveillance systems. The cost alone would be too onerous. China is usually considered our most threatening adversary, but its military budget is not much more than one-tenth of ours.

In spite of our own weaponry outlays, we have managed a
25 percent drop in defense spending since 1990, a major con-
tributor to the fact that government spending growth overall has
slowed for the first time in seven decades.

There are other salutary signs. Household incomes and savings are on the rise. Welfare rolls are shrinking. Crime rates have
dropped dramatically. Record numbers are entering college.

Each piece of good news adds to the confidence of the business community, consumers, and investors. With our solid
growth, low unemployment, tame inflation, and budget equilib-
rium, the entire industrialized world now looks at America as the
paradigm to emulate.

MILLENNIUM À LA AMERICA

The world admires more than our economic model. "We live in
an American age," Josef Joffe, an editor and columnist who lives
in Munich, wrote in the New York Times. "Are people risking
death on the high seas to get into China? . . . How many people
want to dress and live like the Japanese? . . . How many are willing to go for an MBA at Moscow U?" One would have to look
to the Roman Empire, Joffe suggests, to find a time when one culture so dominated the world.

The young abroad walk around in Levis and DKNY T-
shirts, and listen to and watch American movies, TV shows, and
CDs. Seventy million non-American households now get MTV.
Basketball has edged out soccer as the world's most popular
sport, according to a survey of 24,000 teenagers around the
world. People everywhere now "prefer Coke to tea, Nikes to san-
dals, Chicken McNuggets to rice, credit cards to cash," notes
Morgan Stanley Dean Witter economist Joseph Quinlan.
Billboards along the road to the Hanoi airport in Vietnam, our
once deadly enemy, now proclaim "Welcome to the world of
VISA" and "Coke welcomes you to Hanoi." So many products

today have no local coloration. Companies can confidently promote global brands and be well received.

The American way is now felt to be the way of the future. As the world modernizes, it Americanizes. Many non-Americans regret and resent this fact, though most see it as a sign of hope that our spirit of individualism, independence, and enterprise will replace their stultifying obsessions with tradition, order, and social hierarchy.

Most critically, English has become *the* first language of commerce and science. It is taught to teenagers in Japanese and European schools, and to aspiring business executives in language classes around the globe. The availability of English-speaking workers has been a boon to American companies. They can tap into a labor pool anywhere on the map.

More importantly, those living overseas can understand our song lyrics, films, and advertising slogans. The packs of Wrigley's chewing gum sold abroad carry the required ingredients lists translated into the various native languages, but the American brand names remain, universally recognized. (How could you find foreign equivalents for "Juicy Fruit" anyway?) Foreigners can relate to the messages from America they are constantly receiving. Admiring what they see and hear, they want to adopt, or adapt to, the American lifestyle. The hegemony of American culture obviously bodes well for the continued success of U.S. products on global markets.

ENTREPRENEURIAL DRIVE

Risk-taking seems to come more naturally to Americans. Maybe entrepreneurship is the inheritance of our frontier forefathers. Our economic growth is constantly fueled by the creation of new businesses. If someone has an invention of value or a concept with promise, the money will be there to finance its launching. Venture capital is simply not as abundant elsewhere in the world.

Venturesome spirits and funding have created the high-tech powerhouses of Silicon Valley, Boston's Route 128, North Carolina's Research Triangle, and many other similar offshoots. That same restless start-up energy now permeates our entire business culture, Americans have "that maddening can-do attitude that often drives foreigners insane," writes Peter Schwartz and Peter Leyden in *Wired*. Our New World mentality—the sense that we are not shackled by outmoded traditions but are ready to recreate ourselves as the world turns—has always given us a freshness, adaptability, and dynamism that older societies have recognized and often envied.

OPEN OPPORTUNITY

America has other intrinsic advantages over Japan and Europe that make its companies preferred contenders. Its very geography is one. With a density of population about 10 times ours, Japan finds it difficult to accept immigrants. Immigrants bring America the labor, skilled and unskilled, for a growing economy, as well as additional consumers to help sustain that growth. Our overall population isn't as young as Southeast Asia's, but it is younger than Japan's or Europe's. We have a new generation of workers to train in the emerging technologies, an employed base to support welfare programs, and proportionately fewer aged citizens to support.

Many of the advantages the United States enjoys over its key rivals will not last forever. Although Japanese and European companies are making advancements in the way of restructuring, American companies are already fit and trim, having undergone restructurings of their own. This gives them a competitive advantage in the global marketplace for the foreseeable future. Our leading multinationals certainly have an enormous head start in building the worldwide infrastructures that have taken many years and billions of dollars to assemble. A number of Japanese and European companies have made parallel efforts, which must be considered by investors. But the roster of outstanding successes, and those best positioned for the Golden Age, is dominated by American names. These are the companies investors should turn to first.

CHAPTER ELEVEN

CONSIDER THE ALTERNATIVES

THERE'S SMALL CHOICE IN ROTTEN APPLES.

WILLIAM SHAKESPEARE

I do not claim that American multinational growth stocks are the only way to make money in the stock market. I simply believe they are far and away the best investments to own in the early stages of the Golden Age of Capitalism. For the sake of argument, let's take a look at some of the other investment styles and approaches to see why.

MOMENTUM INVESTING

Momentum investors go with the flow. They buy whatever companies have earnings, at least in the short term, that are not just growing or projected to grow, but growing at an accelerated rate quarter by quarter. They also want price momentum, stocks with increasingly broad investor endorsement. One can play the same game with industries or sectors, rather than individual stocks.

Prices or P/E ratios, whether absolute or relative to the market, are of little concern. The force is with these stocks for the moment. Who cares if they're overvalued? Momentum will carry them still higher. Or so proponents of this style contend.

At the first hint of trouble—when there is even a rumor that earnings could disappoint—the momentum player sells spontaneously and looks for the next comet. Momentum portfolios turn over two, three, or even four times a year.

The momentum practitioner is akin to the chartist (one who examines stock price charts), at least as far as judging a stock's market behavior is concerned. These managers also claim to look at company fundamentals, to assure themselves that the predicted earnings are likely to come through. One has to doubt, however, that a person with such a short-term interest in the company would bother to learn much about it. Why go to the trouble of finding out if the company is really good, as long as enough investors this week are convinced it's terrific?

Betting on companies the handicappers like can work very well for a time, particularly in a prolonged bull market when no major unpleasantness interrupts the upward sweep, when speculation abounds, and the general euphoria sends some stocks to excessive heights. Most importantly, it works when billions of dollars flow into momentum funds, serving to self-generate performance. As the name suggests, momentum can carry you far. This was certainly the case in 1999, and through April 2000.

But when things go wrong, often they go *very* wrong. When investors fall into the game of extrapolating accelerating earnings out into the future, they bid stocks up to prices that are ridiculously ahead of reality. Since these are not, on the whole, mature companies with a nice monopoly and recurring revenues, the earnings don't materialize. Even a minor disappointment to expectations sends all of these managers piling up to the exits at once. Drops of 30 to 50 percent in a single day are not unusual. The momentum works in reverse. Such was the case from mid-2000 through 2001.

Momentum investing is important to recognize because it made headlines for much of the 1990s. Some major practitioners realized outsized returns for several years and were put on pedestals by the press. They were portrayed as flamboyant and gifted, not unlike rock stars, and the publicity drew a large following. Then came the unraveling. Once this happened, investors began to appreciate managers who were more like symphony orchestra conductors than pop performers. They revered those who were serious, hard working, disciplined, and dedicated to enduring themes, rather than devotees of improvisation and the faddish. Long-term investors, interested in sustainable, not necessarily accelerating, earnings growth gained new respect.

In my mind, betting on presumptive winners, with no long-term perspective or reliance on company fundamentals, comes very close to pure speculation. It is particularly appalling that many institutions, whose time horizons may be infinite, are also drawn to this quick-fix approach to the market. As for individual investors, they play the nerve-wracking game at a handicap, since they are not privy to the Street analysts who feed the professionals with minute-by-minute earnings forecasts. Besides, how many people consistently make money at the racetrack? Not many.

VALUE INVESTING

The value investor is a growth investor's chief philosophical rival. A value investor looks for companies that are "cheap." Such companies are usually bargain priced because their earnings haven't been growing. This type of investor is attracted to stocks selling at less than the underlying company's assets. This includes "hidden" assets, such as appreciated property carried on the books at cost. Value investors may also seek out businesses with declining earnings that are poised for a turnaround; those that operate in a cyclical industry whose fortunes are reviving; or those candidates so cheap they are likely to be taken over.

Sometimes the value investor is wrong, and there is no turnaround or corporate buyer. The stock is cheap for a good reason and deserves to stay that way. If the value investor is right, the stock will bounce back toward "true value." Sometimes the wait can be long. Once this value is realized, the value investor sells and looks for another bargain.

The growth stock investor, on the other hand, doesn't have to keep unearthing hidden values and little understood businesses. He (or she) pays more for tried-and-true growers. If he is selective, he has virtual assurance that the growth will continue and his expectations will be met. He can be a long-term investor. Over time, he can make 10 times his money in a stock, or even more.

Don't just take my word for it that value investing is inferior to a well-reasoned growth approach. William J. O'Neil, founder of *Investor's Business Daily* and a highly recognized historian of the stock market, opined the following in an article titled "Why Growth Stocks Are Usually Best," published in the paper on October 29, 2001:

"If you choose to invest in individual stocks and you're not a professional investor, I firmly believe it is better for you to avoid the value approach and learn to invest in the very best growth companies. Buy corporations that lead their particular industries in sales, earnings, profit margins, and return on equity. Buy companies that are gaining market share on their competitors . . . In all my years in the business, and knowing thousands of investors, I have never known a non-professional who produced really outstanding results using the value method. I know there have been a few people out there; I've just never met them."

A number of institutional investors claim to straddle both major camps. They say they buy growth companies, but only at a "reasonable price." They refuse to "overpay," which sounds eminently responsible. But when you look at their portfolios, you see few, if any, of the names leading America into a global economy.

Their ingrained value bias will not allow them to pay even the most reasonable premium for superior growth. They have an aversion to high multiple stocks, in absolute, no matter that those multiples are modest relative to the companies' growth rates or historical valuations. Paying up for Wal-Mart, Automatic Data Processing, or Abbott Laboratories simply goes against the grain. They instead hope to find cheaper growth companies that are not yet widely discovered. In my opinion, however, these won't be the prime beneficiaries of the profitable environment ahead.

Warren Buffett started his investing life in the value camp. He was a devoted follower of Benjamin Graham, undoubtedly because he was (rightly so) unwilling to pay the huge premiums then accorded to the best-recognized growth companies. But he has made concentrated investments in Coca-Cola, Gillette, and McDonald's. Buffett subsequently sold his stake in McDonald's, but later called that move a "mistake." Has Buffett decided that some of the best values lie in those companies ideally equipped to deal with a global economy?

SMALL COMPANIES

The conventional wisdom is that small companies—usually defined as those with a market capitalization of under $1 billion—can growth faster than large companies, and therefore offer the greatest appreciation potential.

I don't deny the allure of small companies, with their fresh products, services, images, marketing concepts, and other innovative twists that may turn them into outsized winners. We should all have invested in Intel, Wal-Mart, and Home Depot when they were just starting out.

Unfortunately, it's extremely difficult to identify which small companies will succeed and which will fall prey to the challenges of growth, competition (if you have a great idea, someone else is sure to imitate it), changes in taste, financing tangles, management blowups, and the plethora of other problems that face young enterprises. More small companies fail than succeed. When you buy a Johnson & Johnson or Merck, you know their adolescent growing pains are far behind them.

Successful companies don't stay small-caps. The managers of small-cap portfolios who remain true to their mandate are forced to sell off their most successful investments. Consultants to pension funds and other institutions demand it in order to maintain diversification guidelines. Such asset allocation strategies are doomed to produce mediocrity, in my view, but such has been the tyranny of the consultants to large institutional investors.

If you agree that the most exciting potential now lies in marketing to billions of new global consumers, you must invest in large companies. Small companies, by definition, don't have the resources to do the job. Just building a telecommunications network to connect a company's employees worldwide is prohibitively expensive for a young enterprise with global ambitions. The companies I want to own already have all of their scaffolding in place and the capital to build upon it.

Size brings decided advantages. Large companies can make strategic acquisitions. They can spread many of their costs—research and development, marketing, and advertising—over a larger revenue base. They have more clout with suppliers and can offer customers a greater array of services. The lower costs associated with large-scale operations create not only higher returns, but also barriers to entry, which help sustain those high returns. It is easier to get bigger than to get big.

There is little point, then, to taking the risk associated with newer enterprises. You can buy 10 small company stocks and figure that two of them will go out of business, five will be average performers, two will do better-than-average, and one will be a big winner. At the end of the day, you will not have as much money in your account as if you had simply invested in a select group of multinationals which, on average, are increasing earnings by 10 to 15 percent (or more) a year.

QUANTITATIVE INVESTING

A quantitative approach to equities takes available data about companies and their stock price history, asks a computer to massage that data, and comes up with a ranking of the stocks that are purportedly most likely to outperform. No analyst ever calls on management to make subjective judgments—decisions are wholly generated by a computer. Rocket science? Perhaps. At least that is what we are asked to believe. The practitioners are constantly in their laboratories, fine-tuning their algorithms.

To a large degree, the quants—as they are called in the industry—are the offspring of the chartists. But computers can do so much more than graph paper. In a sense, both the chartists and the quants are heirs of the alchemists, searching for the key that will unlock the door to certain riches. Often, the searcher discovers one variable with amazing predictive power, which maddeningly then fails because other critical interactive factors have evolved. An investment firm should be a place of judgment, not mindless formula.

The quants have a mixed record. Some have done poorly; others have turned in respectable results. Whatever they may achieve—and, after all, a computer has managed to beat the world's chess champion—they will be hobbled in the era we have entered for one fundamental reason: their programs are built on data that reflect past corporate and market behavior. The Golden Age is a new, unprecedented phenomenon. Historical ratios and patterns are no guide. What is needed is the ability to identify those companies with sustainable growth rates that are extending their global reach. These are critical factors that quantitative methods cannot reveal. A quant approach may earn modest returns, but leadership will lie elsewhere.

STOCK PICKERS AND OPPORTUNISTS

There is another breed of investor who downplays categories and prides himself or herself in being a stock picker who will use growth or value criteria, momentum studies, charts, quant rankings, or all of the above to ferret out winners. The size or type of company is irrelevant. The only thing that matters is having a nose for what will go up. Somewhat mysteriously, a combination of knowledge, experience, and instinct will lead them to the big movers.

Stock pickers have become the stars of the business. Ordinary managers need disciplines and systems, they say. These folks operate on talent—nay, genius. Their pictures adorn glossy magazine pages. I won't say there aren't people with a special gift for investing. But after decades of practicing this profession, I do wonder how many Peter Lynches (the renowned former Fidelity Magellan manager) there truly are. Anyone in my business could name countless managers who were touted in the press after two or three years of good numbers and then proceeded to stumble over the next two or three years. Many were never able to shine again. If some are blessed with an innate genius for stock selection, why do the periodicals need to keep changing their lists of the "best" managers and mutual funds? The same is true of the Wall Street gurus and investment newsletter writers who predict market turns. A few have been right more often than wrong, but only a few. Most hot hands turn cold before long. Maybe even Peter Lynch would have disappointed if he hadn't taken an early retirement.

For my part, I believe in having an investment philosophy, a system for carrying it out, and the discipline to stick with it. Over time, that will work wonders. My philosophy is that it's smarter to pick good businesses than trying to pick trendy stocks.

ALTERNATIVE INVESTMENTS

Aside from dabbling in the commodities and currency markets, aggressive investors approach the equity markets through a combination of options and futures; program trading, which involves arbitrage between futures and the underlying markets; strategic asset allocation, which is a refined form of timing; various long-short programs; and other so-called sophisticated strategies. These ingenious inventions flow continuously from various Wall Street and sundry investment think tanks.

Few individual investors become involved in these strategies unless they are either rich enough to hire the hedge fund managers who use them, or foolish enough to get caught up in the options, futures, and commodities markets on their own. For the most part, these more abstruse approaches have been championed by pension funds and endowments that consider them to be state-of-the-art. To my way of thinking, the institutions should know better. These are high-risk strategies, high-cost to execute, and trading oriented. Such maneuvers have nothing to do with investing, and they are wholly unnecessary, since a commitment to the right companies for the era before us will supply better returns without using a battery of probability theorists.

INTERNATIONAL AND EMERGING MARKETS INVESTING

If so many opportunities have been opened by the demise of communism, the advent of globalization, and the emergence of a vast middle class in the developing world, why not invest directly in those overseas companies?

Personal finance pundits often loudly inform us that since many of these economies are growing twice as fast as our own, anyone who can stand a little volatility would be a fool not to send some portion of their money to the developing world. Admittedly, it would be difficult to pick and choose among companies in the Philippines, Turkey, and Chile on one's own, even with the help of a friendly broker. As a result, it has been a compelling story, albeit with a mostly unhappy ending.

Emerging markets were a great place to be in 1993, when the average gain on the few funds around then was a whopping 72 percent. This short-term performance convinced investors to send billions to the funds. They've been a huge disappointment ever since.

Currency and market collapses began in Thailand in 1998 and spread quickly to Indonesia, Malaysia, South Korea, and elsewhere in Asia. This debacle infected almost every emerging market country, with nasty consequences in markets as distant as Brazil and Russia. American companies have seized the opportunities created by these crises to expand and strengthen their positions abroad, at the expense of the local operators.

Developing nations have always been dangerous investment markets, even for sophisticated professionals. Currency fluctuations and devaluations are a constant worry. Companies scattered around the globe are difficult and expensive to research. The markets are thin. It's hard to accumulate a large position without progressively pushing up the price of acquired shares, and difficult to sell without drastically knocking the prices down. The markets are frighteningly volatile. Recurrent drops of 50 percent or more are common. It's tough to get reliable information about companies, especially since accounting practices differ from our own. Poor regulation, cross ownership of shares among companies, and insider trading—often perfectly legal in these countries—distort values. And there is always political risk, such as the possible overthrow of a government and the establishment of a regime hostile to a free market, resulting in a collapse of stability and share prices. Though shareholders don't have to deal directly with these realities, investors in emerging markets mutual funds don't completely escape them.

Consumers in the developing countries are there all right. Their numbers are growing, and the opportunities are real. But investors can profit from these markets better and more safely by putting their money in those U.S. multinationals that sell to these countries on a daily basis. That way there's no worry about liquidity, securities market regulation and supervision, disclosure, accounting practices, revolutions, or volatile local exchanges. On average, the management fees for emerging markets mutual funds are double those of U.S. stock funds. One knows, furthermore, that with globalization and the revolution in mass communications, consumption patterns are converging around the world. The American product, not the local variety, is almost universally the consumer's first choice. Besides, if the companies you invest in operate in multiple countries, trouble in even several areas won't shatter the bottom line.

In short, strong U.S. global companies till the same fields as international and emerging markets funds, but with far more stability and assurance. With the preeminent position American companies enjoy, one has to question the need to look for opportunities even in the developed economies of Europe and Japan, or through the auspices of international or global mutual funds.

The standard argument for investing in foreign markets is that they don't behave in tandem with our, and that diversification lowers total portfolio volatility. This may have once been valid, but now that investors in U.S. stocks are the same people who have poured money into foreign bourses, investor euphoria or panic are reflected universally. The Dow Jones Industrial Average and most foreign exchanges plunged in tandem in 1973–74, October 1987 (when the Hong Kong market shut down for seven days, and then opened 33 percent lower), in the summer of 1998, and more recently during the inflating in 1999 and subsequent popping of the Internet and technology bubble in 2000–01. When it comes to foreign investing, *Forbes* columnist A. Gary Schilling has observed, "When you really need the diversification, it lets you down. When markets crash, they crash in unison."

Nevertheless, financial advisers still routinely tout the wisdom of "spreading risk" by investing in the category labeled "international," including the emerging markets. "Profits don't accrue to categories,"writes Roger Lowenstein in *The Wall Street Journal*. "They are earned, singly, by companies." U.S. multinationals offer all the diversity you could want, by industry, size, sensitivity to business cycles and interest rates, geographical markets, and so forth. "You can lead a happy investment life without leaving home," concludes Lowenstein.

INDEXING

The more widely it has been publicized that most professional equity managers do not outperform the "averages," usually meaning the Standard & Poor's 500 index, the more money that has flowed into index funds. These passive vehicles are run by computer and reflect the performance of the S&P, minus the usually small management fees. During the long bull market, which dates back to 1982, the index proved a persistent provider of gratifying returns. On average, active equity managers—inevitably holding some cash, bearing higher turnover and transaction costs, charging steep management fees, and pursuing a tendency to look for fast-growers among small- and mid-sized companies outside of the S&P 500—fell behind the index and index funds.

If you believe, as I do, that the key to investment success is basically no more complicated than buying great businesses and being patient, then one must acknowledge two important virtues of indexation. First, indices such as the S&P 500 are comprised of the best companies among a very broadly diversified list of industries. It is constantly culled of its losers and refreshed with new winners. Therefore, it generally represents the cream of the crop of corporate America. Second, indices are most commonly used as a core holding in a long-term financial plan. Accordingly, they are *held* and therefore derive the vital compounding benefit that accrues to the patient investor.

But indexation is not the optimum choice for the Golden Age of Capitalism. As I have stressed, many large companies, even the multinationals, are going to lose out in a competitive environment. The S&P is comprised of many well-established, prestigious companies. But these "blue chips" have life cycles, and many in the index are well into maturity. Their days of vigorous growth are arguably behind them. Why not concentrate on the select vanguard of companies within the S&P that are still vigorously positioned to thrive in this new era?

What's more, in recent years the S&P has become more heavily weighted in technology companies, whose earnings predictability are erratic at best. This big technology weighting helped propel the S&P ever higher during the late 1990s, as tech mania swept the nation. But those "good old days," where technology stocks skyrocketed regardless of the fundamental realities, are now gone. Over the past decade, earnings of the premier growth companies I profile in this book have been growing, on average, at an annual rate well over twice the S&P 500. Yet, on average, their P/E multiples have little or no price premium (see Figure 5.1 on page 28).

Ironically, the S&P 500 has become a victim of its own huge success. The flow of trillions of dollars into the S&P and its look-alikes—including all of the portfolios that closely match the S&P—have made their success a self-fulfilling prophecy. But this phenomenon can persist only so long before investors become less willing to assume the price risk now inherent in the S&P and its mimics. The S&P's PEG ratio (P/E divided by the sustainable growth rate) *exceeds* the PEG ratio of sustainable growth companies at their most extreme overvaluation in the not-so-nifty early 1970s.

It is only common sense that a concentrated portfolio of carefully selected companies that are historically undervalued is likely to outperform a broadly diversified index that is historically highly valued over time. Why keep your nest egg invested in anything else?

Chapter Twelve

PUTTING IT TOGETHER

DON'T TRY AND FIGURE OUT WHAT THE MARKET IS DOING. FIGURE
OUT BUSINESSES YOU UNDERSTAND AND CONCENTRATE.
DIVERSIFICATION IS PROTECTION AGAINST IGNORANCE. BUT IF YOU
DON'T FEEL IGNORANT, THE NEED FOR IT GOES DOWN
DRASTICALLY."

JOHN MAYNARD KEYNES

You now know how to recognize the strongest companies for the years ahead: Those with niches dominant enough in their markets to sustain price levels that assure a healthy profit margin, products or services that are constantly consumed and reordered, and the ability to sell those products and services to a swelling global constituency. In-depth profiles of specific companies are ahead, but I bet you can already name many of them.

Every investor, whatever his or her strategy, must decide whether to buy stocks either directly or through a mutual fund. It's certainly fine to do both. One can have a core exposure to the equity market through a fund or funds, and also invest in those individual companies you find to be particularly attractive. Conversely, you can assemble a central stock portfolio on your own and use funds for special sectors or asset classes.

Judging by the enormous amounts of money that have poured into mutual funds in recent years, most people don't feel they have the time, interest, or aptitude to manage a portfolio of individual stocks on their own. They prefer to leave that to a professional, which usually means a mutual fund. The very wealthy can command their own separate account at a counseling firm with a steep minimum. Fortunately, most such firms (including ours) also offer mutual funds that are available to even the smallest investor following a similar discipline and owning mainly the same stocks.

There is much to be said for investing on one's own, aside from the attraction of being a fascinating avocation. Primarily, it is *your* money, and it is satisfying to take charge of it. Should you decide to go that route, I'd like to offer some observations and advice based on my many years in this business.

The do-it-yourselfer has several advantages over the fund manager. The latter, constantly ranked and appraised, is under tremendous pressure that can unnerve his or her better judgment. It is hard for a manager not to think more about the fund's short-term performance than the long-term performance of his portfolio companies. When you run your own portfolio, you can be patient with the companies you believe in. Since so many of the professionals these days tend to dump anything with a near-term problem, the private investor who maintains a long-term perspective can often pick up favored companies at discount prices.

A prime example was health care stocks in 1993, when the first Clinton Administration's "reform" package was submitted to the nation. Nervous institutions immediately dumped shares in stocks like Merck, Pfizer, and Abbott Laboratories, and prices took a beating. When Wal-Mart's earnings growth paused in the early 1990s as it bore the initial expenses of expanding outside the United States, impatient professionals switched to other stocks with more immediately happy prospects. Tiffany, Colgate-Palmolive, Wrigley, and other global powerhouses met a similar fate during the Asian crisis of 1998, and again during the market correction of 2000–01.

Direct investors can concentrate their portfolios on the companies they feel most strongly about and perhaps know personally from their own business or professional contacts. Funds that gather hundreds of millions of dollars are forced to diversify ever more widely. The average equity fund has about 120 stocks. This is an invitation to mediocrity. We have been told so often that diversification lowers risk that we tend to believe the more of it, the better. "One good share is safer than ten bad ones," John Maynard Keynes once commented. Consultant Charles Ellis also has noted that when you own dozens of stocks, you dilute your knowledge of each and get too dependent on the research and judgments of others. "A long list of holdings," he remarked, "is no more 'portfolio diversification' than a huge pile of stones is Chartres Cathedral."

It would indeed be daunting if you felt you had to make choices among 15,000 publicly traded companies. But the kind of core portfolio I am recommending requires your consideration of less than two dozen companies—all big, well-known, and widely followed. Information about them is readily available. Stories on them appear constantly in the press. You can consult the *Value Line Investment Survey* at your library for recent progress reports, and check the Internet for more up-to-date news.

I increasingly find Wall Street research to be of little help— and often harmful—to the long-term investor. Street analysts are caught up in the same short-term mania as the money managers they serve. More and more they focus on price targets for the next quarter or two, and give short shrift to fundamental trend analysis. Successful stock picks for the next reporting period are what win them a place on *Institutional Investor* magazine's All-America Research Team, thus assuring a premium salary. What they should be doing is spotting the trends—and changes in trends—that may not show up in stock prices (positively or negatively) for quite some time.

For that reason, I participate in the telephone conference calls regularly sponsored by the companies in which I invest. You can, too. As a result of the SEC's Regulation FD, which requires companies to give full disclosure of material events to all investors (not just analysts and institutions), most leading companies have been Webcasting their quarterly earnings calls with the analyst community over the Internet. I don't trust the analysts and members of the media to be reliable filters of this information. Again, their short-term bias compels them to treat a company's announcement that it is stepping up capital outlays, arranging a strategically sound acquisition, or making some other commitment that will dilute earnings—even modestly—for the coming quarter as bad news. Developments that lead these analysts to downgrade stocks are confidence-inspiring to the long-term investor, since they bolster the company's ability to *sustain* earnings growth into the future.

This happens all the time. In 1993, analysts were down on State Street because its heavy spending on technology penalized near-term earnings. But State Street so successfully raised the competitive bar that other financial institutions—BankAmerica, J.P. Morgan, and Morgan Stanley among them—got out of the global custody business, abdicating the field to State Street. In 1997, Pfizer was penalized when it announced an anticipated temporary narrowing of profit margins as it expanded its sales force in advance of expected FDA approval of several blockbuster drugs, including the sensationally successful Viagra. Starbucks earned a thumbs-down when it revealed that the costs of introducing a new ice cream line nationally, starting up operations in Asia, and acquiring the United Kingdom-based Seattle Coffee Company would cause a moderate slowdown in its otherwise heady earnings growth. Even though these moves were critical to future growth, analysts and money managers reacted nearsightedly, creating buying opportunities for anyone with a modicum of vision and patience.

The truth is that people in my line of work identify few analysts we really value and respect. I have repeatedly seen analysts downgrade a stock—the same one they have just been loudly touting—from a buy to a hold or sell *after* the company announces some piece of bad news. What's more, the downgrades are issued before the market opens, and the previous day's closing price is used as the exit price when the analyst or his firm later publishes the performance of its recommended list.

THE BUILDING BLOCKS

Few individual investors have sufficient assets available for investing to warrant holding all 20 companies that we will be examining later in the book. Half will probably do. Such a portfolio would provide sufficient diversification by types of businesses and markets. (Even the pharmaceuticals have such varied product lines, their fortunes don't normally correlate.) The unexpected can happen to even the best companies, and a reasonable level of diversification lends shelter from company shocks, market whims, and an uncomfortable level of volatility. If you don't have at least $100,000 to invest in common stocks, you have little flexibility in managing a diversified portfolio, and are probably best off in mutual funds.

In choosing stocks from a list of favored candidates for your portfolio, you must decide which issues are currently most attractive, based on the companies' recent growth rates and current market prices. There is always a trade-off between the two. Remember that I said the price-to-earnings multiples of leading global growth stocks may look high in the absolute, but not relative to the rate of growth of those earnings, particularly when the growth rate is compared to that of the overall market. Examining and comparing recent and projected growth rates and current multiples of earnings will lead you to those companies that are most attractively priced at the moment.

Any investor can make this analysis, buy 10 or so companies, and simply hold on, selling only when he or she believes a company has finally saturated its markets, lost its edge, or when the stock's price has risen to a level where continued superior returns are doubtful. The proceeds would then be switched to a more attractive issue.

Other investors will try to enhance their returns regularly by shifting a portion of their money as valuations change, lightening up on stocks that have risen to the upper end of their premium-to-the-market range, and weighting more heavily those issues that have lagged. Even when a company's revenues and earnings progress in relatively steady fashion, its stock price will fluctuate considerably. Relative attractiveness is in constant flux, and the astute manager can take advantage of the changing trade-offs between growth and value.

Understand that I am not endorsing a trading regimen. These shifts make sense only periodically, and usually involve only a part of a position. No matter how sophisticated the valuation tools and methods, no one can predict stock prices. The market can continue to push up a stock that by reasonable measures has moved above its "fair" price, while stubbornly neglecting a stock that seems undervalued. You don't want to sell your entire position in a company you like just because its stock price has seemingly gotten a bit ahead of itself, though you might ease up a bit. These favored companies are long-term holdings, and the investor's annual turnover rate should remain low. If the shares are held outright, rather than in your IRA or 401(k) plan, the lower long-term capital gains rates make this resolve even more compelling.

Fine tuning a portfolio to ease up on those stocks that have climbed sharply in price to more heavily weight those believed to have more upside potential is a contribution the mutual fund manager is paid to make. In this regard, he or she has an advantage over the individual investor—at least if his or her record has been good enough to attract fresh dollars. If Pfizer's stock has been in great favor with investors and Merck's stock performance has been ho-hum, it may be an opportune time to allocate incoming cash flow to Merck. The manager, unlike most individual investors, doesn't have to sell some Pfizer, which still looks good, to raise the bet on Merck.

Being in charge of your portfolio also has important tax advantages over mutual fund investing. You can time your transactions to offset losses, or postpone gains until they are long-term or realized in a later year.

Many investors would consider no other course but self-management. They have been investing on their own for years, enjoy the research and satisfaction of running their own show, and are convinced they can do a better job than the mutual fund manager who has to worry about shareholder inflows and outflows, a cash balance to cover possible redemptions, the restrictions imposed by the fund's mandate, and the pressures of having one's results posted daily. Professional managers, seeing the same Street research and conditioned to the common shortsighted responses, tend to buy and sell in unison. Sir John Templeton sagely noted, "It is impossible to produce a superior return unless you do something different from the majority." The fact that most equity mutual funds underperform a passive index fund further convinces individual investors that they can do as well as, if not better than, the pros. Any experienced investor convinced of the arguments of this book would have no trouble constructing and monitoring a portfolio from among the companies I recommend for the *core* of your nest egg.

Generally speaking, when choosing stocks to buy or weight more heavily, a contrarian bent pays off. In the late 1990s, the press began slamming McDonald's, calling it a giant that had lost its way. McDonald's management and board did not go into denial about their company's problems. The lagging stock price of McDonald's alone alerted them to that. A good business can fix its problems, and McDonald's is a very good business. Burger King would give anything to have its international infrastructure. Some of the problems at McDonald's were internal and could be dealt with. Among the initiatives, management decisions have been decentralized, the menu has been revamped, and the food preparation process has been overhauled.

But a lot of it had to do with exogenous factors that were cyclical in nature or completely out of the company's control, such as the temporary near panic in Europe over mad cow and hoof and mouth diseases. The same is true of Coke. Coke recently had some internal problems it was forced to address. But much of its difficulty came by virtue of the fact that it operates in 120 different countries, each of which faces its own unique challenges. Historically, we've seen that the best time to buy these stocks is when the flak and cyclical problems are at their worst.

I have stressed the opportunities of companies able to reach an ever-expanding global market. But one should not choose portfolio companies solely on the basis of which receive the highest percentage of total revenues from abroad. Global reach is one criterion among many. Wrigley, Colgate, and Gillette are truly global companies. Some, like Wal-Mart, Staples, and Starbucks, are building their presence abroad. Others, including Home Depot, have only recently taken their first steps onto foreign shores, but the potential is genuine and immense. As important as a worldwide infrastructure is, you are not assembling an international or global portfolio, but a *growth* portfolio.

Indeed, I can provide no checklist of ratios you can refer to, with the importance to assign to each. That would be convenient, but unrealistic. There are too many variables, whose importance differs from industry to industry and company to company, and they are in constant motion. If there were a perfect portfolio today, it would be imperfect a week from today. I can offer you a *philosophy*, but not a *formula*.

There is one number worth monitoring, however: a company's reinvestment rate. As was emphasized earlier, sustainable growth is supported by a high level of reinvestment of profits back into the business. A deteriorating reinvestment rate, for example, would have tipped investors off to the fact that Dun & Bradstreet and Reader's Digest had lost momentum in the mid-1990s.

Of course it is desirable to buy stocks at the lower end of their valuation range. But the timing of purchases is not a critical factor for the long-term investor in companies whose earnings are rising steadily at a double-digit rate. Anyone who constructs a portfolio from among such companies will come out a winner.

THE MUTUAL FUND ALTERNATIVE

Whatever the advantages of managing one's own portfolio, many feel they have no aptitude for, and little interest in, such an assignment. They want mutual funds to do the job for them.

Mutual funds are certainly a simple and convenient way to be involved in the stock market. You gain instant diversification, albeit perhaps more than you would like. Someone trained and experienced in securities valuation is spending his or her days keeping on top of earnings announcements, analysts' reports, and stock price movements. You can check on that person's job performance in the morning newspaper. Dividends and capital gains distributions can be automatically reinvested, and regular statements simplify record keeping and tax reporting.

There are hundreds of large-cap growth funds—the likeliest general category in which to find a suitable core long-term holding—but not many of them focus on sustainable growth companies. Any fund with an average annual portfolio turnover rate of more than 30 percent would be scratched off my list of possibilities. A higher turnover rate signals a manager who chases stocks, not one who invests in good companies. While modest adjustments to the weightings of holdings in response to changes in market valuations can be advantageous, a portfolio of proven growth companies needs little alteration.

Turnover is expensive. One of my quarrels with the increasingly short-term perspective of institutions is the cost. The average stock fund, with 80 percent turnover, eats up about 1.4 percent of assets annually in transactions fees, not to mention the possible impact on stock prices when buying and selling large positions. For taxable accounts, high turnover is particularly costly. Sales of appreciated stocks generate capital gains. When stocks are held instead of sold, the money that would have gone to the IRS compounds on the investor's behalf. A 30 percent turnover hurdle alone eliminates a large proportion of growth funds. You can find turnover rates in a fund's prospectus, and through such rating services as Morningstar and Value Line.

Large-cap funds with low turnover and good *long-term* performance are almost certain to own at least a few of the companies I have highlighted. However, four or five in a portfolio of 50 is not what I have in mind. As noted earlier, most funds, feeling they are competing in a 100-yard dash, have little interest in the long-term merits of the kinds of companies I prefer. If these stocks were not too lowly weighted in mutual funds and other institutional portfolios, they wouldn't be as undervalued as they are today.

By looking at a fund's holdings, it is quickly apparent whether its guiding principle leads it to U.S. multinational companies with dominate global brand names and leadership in consumer and business services, or instead to technology stocks, obscure names, or highly volatile issues. If the latter is true, it suggests the manager is looking for companies whose earnings might go up 50 percent in the next 12 months rather than 15 percent annually for the next 12 years. Though I like to believe that the funds I manage follow the philosophy I espouse in the purest form, there are a limited number of other funds whose holdings show this same class of predominant companies. More such funds will no doubt be launched to take advantage of growing perceptions of where the future lies.

Reading the prospectus, annual report, and marketing literature should (and I emphasize "should" because not all fund sponsor materials are as revealing as they might be) also give you a feel for the manager's approach to the equity market. Fund manager interviews in newspapers, business and personal finance magazines, and on the Internet can be particularly enlightening, especially if the interviewer is sharp. You can judge from the responses whether the manager understands the world in terms of the revolutionary changes that have occurred, or if he or she is merely interested in picking the stocks most likely to ring the bell in the next three months.

GETTING THE RIGHT HELP

Given that information about mutual funds—and stocks—is so abundant these days, many investors feel overwhelmed and in need of assistance. Thankfully, there are many qualified brokers and financial advisers who can give you the help you need.

Investment advice is usually an ongoing need, so you should take the time to find someone you trust and work well with. As an investor, your requirements and goals will change as you go through life—a new job, marriage, divorce, babies, graduations, health problems, retirement, an inheritance—all will have an impact on your financial plans. What's more, investment policies need continual review. Usually, only the very young want 100 percent of their invested assets in stocks, and your broker or adviser can help you arrive at an appropriate asset mix for your present and evolving needs. Portfolio adjustments will likely be few, but they do become necessary: Companies and their market valuations change, and mutual funds switch portfolio managers. Every portfolio, even one composed of global leader stocks, must be monitored. An adviser, too, can stiffen the backbone of a nervous investor during market corrections, and remind them during bear markets that the best time to invest is when prices are down.

How do you find a good broker or financial adviser? Ask for recommendations from your accountant, lawyer, and the friends and business contacts you consider knowledgeable about money matters. Some advisers concentrate on specific issues, such as estate planning, and merely offer routine investment help as an adjunct service. Others are more interested in the investment side of the business, and are willing to assist with both direct portfolios and mutual fund selection.

Once you have a name or two, go meet with these professionals. Tell them what you want and expect. You will soon get a sense of whether or not they are right for you. Ask for the names of present clients with whom you can talk. And don't think it will be necessary to go to New York, Chicago, or San Francisco for help. These days, with personal finance being such a growth industry, there are good financial advisers in almost every town.

THE VITAL CORE

However you go about putting together the equity component of your nest egg, its core should be drawn from, or reflect, the companies recommended in Chapter Fourteen (or those you believe show like characteristics). The bulk of one's stock holdings should be devoted to those companies most likely to continue providing superior growth records due to their outstanding strengths in the age we have entered. No other strategy makes as much sense.

For some, the core will be the whole: whatever percentage of their assets they have decided to allocate to common stocks, they will place all of it in major multinational companies with leadership product lines and assured repeat business. Such a portfolio wholly satisfies their philosophy and goals. After all, even with no multiple expansion, the stocks of companies with annual earnings growth in the 15 to 20 percent range will double your money in four-and-a-half to five years. Most of us don't expect better than that. At least we shouldn't.

Other investors, however, will look to these stocks as the heart of their stock exposure—say, 75 percent of their equity allocation—but supplement that foundation with other holdings. They may read about a company with a compelling story or learn about it from friends or business acquaintances, or even know it from personal experience, and want to participate in its projected success. Or they may see promise in a particular market niche and invest in a mutual fund that specializes in small-company stocks, technology, health care, or some foreign region. These supplementary investments will probably be riskier and the goal more short-term.

I wouldn't discourage such ancillary investments. No doubt some of them will pay off handsomely. But the resolve to keep the bulk of one's commitment in this core portfolio shouldn't be compromised. In fact, it is when you have a firm grounding in the types of companies we have considered that you can more confidently wade into riskier territory.

Chapter Thirteen

TIME IS ON YOUR SIDE

A Golden Age for stocks does not assure a smooth ascent to ever-rising peaks. Over time, companies with superior earnings growth, if purchased at rational levels, are almost guaranteed to deliver as promised. That's because higher earnings eventually get translated into higher stock prices. What's more, companies growing faster than the S&P will outperform the index. But the good news will not be delivered each and every week. There are pauses, setbacks, and disappointments in both companies and the market as a whole.

We all know this, yet it's hard to accept. Patience—the ability to wait out the dry spells and concentrate on long-term goals—is a rare commodity among investors. Patience apparently isn't part of our DNA. More than ever in our fast-paced world people are looking for instant gratification. Too often they take reprehensible short-cuts. Why study if you can cheat on exams?

Why work hard if a bit of larceny can bring in the cash faster? Why labor to discover what brings happiness when you can buy drugs? And why wait around for a stock to double in three years when a hot technology number promises to do it in three months?

Impatience explains speculation, high turnover, sector rotation, momentum investing, market timing, and a host of other seductive traps and follies. Fear and greed, the great market movers, are both enemies of patience. Greedy investors chase the fast buck in a rising market and panic into selling when prices fall. They are forever jumping from stock to stock, or fund to fund, or from stocks to cash and back.

Since the stock exchanges first opened, investors dreaming of a short path to riches have tried to forecast the future. Charts, bundles of indicators, and computer-driven models are supposed to signal when to head for the exits before the bear arrives, while ringing a bell once the coast is clear for reentry. I could, from my own experience, add my voice to the chorus of professionals who declare that timing is a fool's game, but there is no better proof than the early 1980s to mid-1990s. In fact, the market did *really* well in the 1980s, although most investors didn't join the party for more than a decade later. Still, some very smart and highly respected market strategists during this period declared, repeatedly and with solemn authority, that the market was overvalued by every measure known to man. Those who listened and were frightened out of the market sat on the sidelines through one of the greatest bull markets in history.

Timers invariably outsmart themselves. They get out too soon and back in too late, cheating themselves of a big part of the market's return, while suffering agonies when the market refuses to behave as the prognosticators predicted. You've probably seen some of the studies. One conducted by the University of Michigan reported that over a 30-year period from the 1960s through the 1990s, 95 percent of the market's cumulative gain came in 1.2

percent of the total trading days. If you missed 90 out of 7,500 days, you made about half as much as you would have if you'd stuck to Treasury bills. For the five years ending December 31, 1996, according to another study, missing just the 10 best trading days of that period would have cut your average annual returns from 12.9 percent to 9.2 percent; if you missed the 20 best days, your return dropped to 6.3 percent; and if you were out of the market the 40 best days, you earned less than 1 percent. "Far more money has been lost by investors preparing for corrections or trying to anticipate corrections," Peter Lynch has noted, "than has been lost in the corrections themselves." A substantial part of almost every bull market's gains occurs in its early days, when the timers are still trying to figure out if the reversal is for real. From August 1982, when the great bull market began, to the end of October 1982—a mere three months—the market soared 42 percent. Clearly, the real risk doesn't lie in being in a falling market, but in being out of a rising market.

It's better to buy stocks as cheap as possible, but the timing of purchases doesn't matter all that much if one's sights are properly set. One study found that if you invested at the onset of all the bear markets since 1945, you would have recouped your losses, on average, in one and a half years. Another 30-year study showed that if you were unlucky enough to have invested in the S&P 500 on its peak day each and every year, your average annual return was 10.6 percent. If you were genius enough to pick the market's absolute low point of the year, you would have made 11.7 percent. The difference from worst to best is that small. Yes, if you were so unfortunate as to buy all of your global leader stocks or growth fund shares near the high end of their valuation cycle, you would need more patience, but toughing out the catch-up phase is vastly preferable to buying companies whose future is bleak. Financial television commentator Louis Rukyeser is fond of saying, "It's time—not timing—that is going to make you rich."

There is also the important matter of taxes. The investor who constantly buys and sells in an effort to market time or grab short-term gains subjects any gains to taxation, and money sent to the IRS instead of compounding in your account makes a startling difference. An investor starting out with $1,000 who brilliantly doubles his or her money every year for 20 years by picking a different stock on January 1 and selling it on December 31 would end up with about $22,000 after paying annual capital gains taxes. If that same investor made a single investment that doubled every year for 20 years, he or she would end up with roughly $700,000 after paying a one-time tax at the same rate. Such is the miracle of compounding, but it only benefits the long-term investor. Almost everyone wags their head in agreement when the familiar adage is sounded: "No one ever went broke taking a profit." Why hasn't it become the accepted wisdom that, "No one has ever gotten rich taking profits too soon?"

Good companies should be kept as long as they remain good companies. George J.W. Goodman, writing under the pen name "Adam Smith" in the classic book *The Money Game*, is right: "More investment mistakes have been made through failure to hold than by failure to get out of premier securities which are believed to be 'overvalued' by the market."

Periods when the overall market is undergoing a correction are actually beneficial to those who adhere to the thesis of this book. In the 18th century, Samuel Johnson recognized this precept when he said, "People need to be reminded more often than they need to be instructed," and in down markets people are reminded (2000–2001, for instance). Shaken, they trend toward back-to-basics investing and away from currently popular approaches based on capitalization size, country of domicile, earnings momentum, this month's "values," market sector rotation, and so-called sophisticated hedging techniques. That trend will obviously and profoundly benefit patient investors in companies with sustainable earnings growth.

But the businesses must be good. One can't be patient of the undeserving. That is the great virtue and comfort of the global powerhouses. One can feel supremely confident in companies with quality products and services, brand-name recognition around the world, exceptional earnings growth records, financial strength, high reinvestment rates, proven ability to develop important new products, state-of-the-art information technology, a global infrastructure, and superior marketing expertise. Furthermore, when you own a diversified portfolio of these companies, or a mutual fund that does, the effects of temporary problems for any one or two names won't be severe. And at the rate the markets for these companies are expanding, not much patience will be required before a comeback.

Interviewers of mutual fund managers almost invariably ask, "What is your sell discipline?" My answer is simple: If you buy the right businesses, you've solved most of your selling problem. The right buying discipline *is* the right selling discipline.

FIXING YOUR SIGHTS

There is only one sure way to acquire patience: Focus on your long-term goals. It isn't easy. You'll certainly get no help from the stock exchanges, which are delighted that trading volume is four times what it was a decade ago. The SEC often pursues a policy of "anything goes as long as it's disclosed," including program trading that creates nothing but heightened volatility.

The media are forever shouting in our ears to take action. If the daily papers aren't enough to keep you in turmoil, you can stay glued to CNN, CNBC, Fox News Channel, MSNBC, or to the many online services such as Microsoft Investor, Motley Fool, MarketEdge, and Yahoo! Finance. Publishers couldn't sell magazines every month if their covers declared "Do Nothing." Your subscription entitles you to fresh advice about what moves to make now. Over and over we see "The Ten Best Stocks to Buy Now" or

"The Best Mutual Funds for the Coming Year." You can be sure that today's "best" will be supplanted by a new list six months down the road.

You have to keep reminding yourself that all of this "advice" is very foolish. A long-term plan means a long-term investment horizon. Concentrate on what your portfolio will be worth in 10 years. An investor should have a horizon of *at least* ten years, which is not unreasonable when your goal is a child's college education or your own retirement. (For institutions, such as perpetual endowments, 10 years is only a moment in a limitless time horizon, which is what makes the short-term orientation of many institutions so outrageous.) Investors who make regular contributions to retirement plans need only remind themselves that during market slumps each dollar invested buys more shares. Investors are manic-depressive, and despite the marvels of medical science, there will be no cure. You've got to learn to control yourself against such mood swings.

"When we watch the market" writes Jason Zweig in *Money*, "much of what seems like news turns out to be nothing more than noise." Or, to quote Peter Lynch again, "Nobody can predict interest rates, the future direction of the economy, or the stock market. Dismiss all such forecasts and concentrate on what's actually happening to the companies in which you're invested."

CHAPTER FOURTEEN

THE TRUSTY 20

I AM EASILY SATISFIED WITH THE VERY BEST.

WINSTON CHURCHILL

To once more hammer home a vital point, the Golden Age of Capitalism will not glitter for all companies, even those with a global presence. Only a small percentage of such firms have a dominating position that bestows pricing power, the kind of products and services that assure repeat sales, and therefore a future of double-digit annual profit growth. I believe it is these companies that are currently among the strongest contenders for market share in a world opened up to both opportunity and rampant competition. By no means is this list all-inclusive. There are other worthy choices. But these are the companies I currently feel most comfortable with.

All are American corporations. Most are already well entrenched on foreign shores. Some, however, have only recently begun to export their specialties. The potential of all, in a global marketplace, is virtually open-ended.

They share a number of defining characteristics, in addition to their franchises, repeat-purchase products, and global muscle. Perhaps the most decisive is their culture. These are aggressive, hard-driving companies determined to beat the competition at every turn, cut costs down to the last nickel, and make sure that one day every person on the globe knows and wants their brands, if they don't already.

A can-do team spirit infuses the whole company, perhaps best epitomized by the weekly pep rallies at Wal-Marts, complete with a rah-rah cheer, a tradition begun by founder Sam Walton. At most of these companies, stock option programs, often reaching down to the lowest employee, buttress loyalty, initiative, and the will to compete. Most of these companies are not unionized, in large part because workers feel no need for such organization.

More than three-quarters of these companies have regularly been buying back the shares of their own stock. This indicates that management thinks their shares are undervalued, regardless of what caveats come out of Wall Street about P/E ratios and other concerns.

Several among this elite group are pharmaceutical and health product houses. This industry sees only boom years ahead. New technologies enable research labs to identify critical variables and screen and test compounds far more readily and efficiently than in the past. Thanks to resultant advances and industry promotions— including the new practice of advertising directly to consumers— drug sales in the United States are rising about 17 percent a year, and profit margins are among the highest of any industry. Globalization has eased the way to disseminate discoveries into all markets. And while life-threatening diseases remain the obvious priority of the research, the industry expects further breakthroughs in life-enhancing medications that treat conditions such as hair loss, wrinkles, obesity, memory loss, arthritic pain, anxiety, and depression. This is a growth industry if there ever was one.

Growth companies have never been considered appropriate for investors looking for income, since most earnings are recycled to fuel further growth, leaving little for distribution as dividends. You will note, however, that many of these companies have been steadily raising their dividends for years. Even though their pay-out ratio from current earnings may still be small, a modest percentage of an ever-growing profit base eventually provides the long-term investor with a handsome income. This leads to a very high percentage return when calculated against your original investment.

A quarter of a century ago, as noted earlier, a group of supposedly super-growth companies was dubbed the "Nifty Fifty." Today I find decidedly less than that number truly qualify as confirmed leaders in a vastly expanded market. I call this hardcore group "The Trusty 20" because it is difficult to envision these companies failing to deliver on their promise. Their track records, proven product appeal, global infrastructures, stated agendas, business tenacity, and demonstrated management skills give me confidence that they will be conquerors of a one-world economy, leaving their rivals far behind.

The fundamentals of these companies tell us they all hold promise for the long term. Of course, they won't all be attractively valued all the time (as explained in the profile on the Walt Disney Company). When managing a stock portfolio, nothing can be carved in stone. Unexpected turns can cause the best company to lose its way or fall behind. A competitor can prove unexpectedly resourceful or fortunate. Valuations can reach limits where other companies offer better risk-reward profiles. Therefore, The Trusty 20—presented now in alphabetical order—cannot be a forever portfolio.

The names in *your* nest egg portfolio will necessarily change over time, but the philosophy that guides it will be valid for at least a decade and probably a good deal longer.

ABBOTT LABORATORIES

A Health Care Arsenal

TICKER SYMBOL: ABT   EXCHANGE: NYSE

Abbott Laboratories is a premier, diversified health care company that discovers, develops, manufactures, and markets a wide range of medical products aimed at preventing, diagnosing, treating, and curing numerous diseases. The company is also a global leader in the area of infant (Similac and Isomil) and adult (Ensure) nutritional supplements. The company's products are used daily by millions of people in more than 130 countries. More than one-third of Abbott's sales come from outside the United States.

The pharmaceuticals business is Abbott's largest and fastest growing. It is focused on five primary therapeutic areas where the company has a competitive advantage: infectious diseases, oncology, neuroscience, diabetes, and immunoscience. Abbott's technology intensive proprietary drug discovery process puts it one step ahead of the competition by enabling the company to quickly screen a myriad of compounds to identify those with the highest potential for drug development. Abbott's discovery system is able to screen more than one million data points per week, accomplishing what used to take six months in ten days. This allows the company to meet its goal of delivering six new compounds into human trials each year.

With its acquisition of Knoll Pharmaceuticals in 2000, the company significantly deepened its product pipeline, increased its research and development capabilities, and became a global leader in monoclonal antibody research. This is among the most promising fields in pharmaceutical science. It allows researchers to target specific proteins on human cells, leading to the rapid development of highly focused and effective treatments with significantly fewer side effects.

Abbott's hospital products division includes drug delivery systems and intensive care, cardiovascular, renal, and oncology products. Most of these brands are not that well known outside of the medical community. Similarly, the company's brands of advanced sensor catheters, intravenous solutions, and electronic drug delivery systems are not household names, although they are the leading products in their categories and respected and relied upon daily by hospital physicians around the world.

The diagnostics division is the world leader in the manufacture and sale of systems and reagents to blood banks, hospitals, laboratories, and consumers. Those products are used to perform tests to detect the presence of diseases, viruses, and abused substances. These products also monitor and control drug levels. Abbott further sells fertility and pregnancy tests.

By investing in Abbott, you can rest assured you have entrusted your money to a broad-based leader in one of the world's most vibrant industries.

CONTACT INFORMATION:

Abbott Laboratories
100 Abbott Park Road
Abbott Park, IL 60064-6400
Telephone: (847) 973-6100
www.abbott.com

AMERICAN INTERNATIONAL GROUP

Risk Manager to the World

TICKER SYMBOL: AIG   EXCHANGE: NYSE

AIG is an extraordinary insurance and financial services behemoth. It generates the highest income of any insurance company in the world. Its shareholder equity, or net worth, is unsurpassed in its industry. It has been chalking up annual earnings gains in the neighborhood of 15 percent for some 25 years, which is rare in any industry, much less for an insurance company.

Although the name AIG might not be familiar, you or your company may well have bought policies from AIG companies such as American General, National Union Fire Insurance of Pittsburgh, American Home Assurance Company, Hartford Steam Boiler, or Lexington Insurance Company. There isn't a kind of insurance its affiliates don't underwrite—life, property and casualty, auto, accident, homeowners, hospitalization, workers compensation, mortgage guaranty, liability, malpractice, aviation, reinsurance, and on down the list—or an insurance broker in the country it doesn't do business with. Currently, the thrust in the United States is to concentrate on the middle-market, defined as smaller and medium-size companies in rapidly growing fields such as technology, information services, and outsourcing.

AIG is probably better known outside the United States, where it derives half of its income from a wide range of commercial and personal insurance products sold through a wide range of distribution channels in more than 130 countries. AIG began life in Shanghai in 1919. Today it is the leading insurer in China and all of Southeast Asia. It started selling policies in Japan a year after World War II ended, before Japan erected barriers against outsiders. Today it is the largest foreign full-service life insurer in that country.

AIG has long been a major player in the institutional pension arena, selling fixed and variable-return retirement packages that supplement or replace government plans in countries that have wholly or partially privatized their pension system such as Chile, Mexico, Peru, Argentina, and Colombia. The 1998 acquisition of Sun America, a leader in annuities and other savings products, significantly bolstered AIG's penetration of the global retirement savings industry.

Every insurance company's profitability rests in large part on the return it earns on its premium-generated assets. AIG has shown skill and resourcefulness in managing its $100-billion-plus portfolio. It has committed more than $1 billion to support corporate buyouts. It buys airplanes and leases them to the world's airlines. In fact, if AIG converted the fleet it owns into an operating airline, it would be the largest in the world.

AIG is an amazing company, constantly expanding its array of products and presence. It has been both a promoter and beneficiary of globalization. It is expertly managed, with a low expense ratio (the lowest among major property-casualty insurers) and a triple-A credit rating. AIG is the kind of opportunistic—in the best sense of the word—company an investor can feel comfortable taking on as his or her long-term business partner.

CONTACT INFORMATION:

American International Group, Inc.
70 Pine Street
New York, NY 10270
Telephone: (212) 770-7000
www.aig.com

AUTOMATIC DATA PROCESSING
Computer Systems for Hire

TICKER SYMBOL: ADP   EXCHANGE: NYSE

Ever since Automatic Data Processing became a publicly traded company in 1961, it has continually reported double-digit earnings growth. It gets more work from its old customers, signs up new customers for its traditional products, expands those products, adds new ones, opens markets overseas, and buys up other companies when the synergies look right.

ADP began as a handler of company payrolls, taking over the burdens of collecting, checking, and calculating employee hours, figuring out all the deductions for taxes, Social Security, Medicare, disability, child support, and wage garnishes, and then printing out the checks. Today ADP processes the paychecks of more than 23 million workers in North America (it is the leader in both Canada and the U.S.) and Europe. It also handles, if the customer elects, the payment of payroll taxes and the sending of year-end tax statements to employees.

But its employer services, which account for more than half of ADP's revenues, now extend well beyond payroll management. It is involved in all employee-related concerns, including unemployment compensation management, employee benefits administration, 401(k) plan administrative services, and travel expense reporting. It can also supply the data and analysis that help human resources directors with absenteeism checks, equal opportunity reports, salary modeling, recruiting, and budgeting. More and more companies, especially small and mid-size firms, find it more efficient and economical to outsource office work rather than build internal staff, constantly update their information systems, and keep abreast of changing regulations. The trend is global.

ADP's second most important division, accounting for about one-quarter of its revenues, works with Wall Street. ADP

Brokerage Services functions as the back office of securities firms, handling all of their securities trading, settlement, and accounting, whether for stocks, bonds, options, or futures, including transactions that involve foreign bourses and multiple currencies. This is a big business: ADP processes about one-fifth of the retail equity transactions in the United States and Canada. It is also the largest processor and provider of shareholder communications.

ADP Dealer Services, contributing about 15 percent of sales, is the world's largest provider of computing, data, and consulting services to auto and truck dealers, with more than 18,000 clients in the United States, Canada, Europe, Asia and Latin America. More than 40 percent of Dealer Services clients are outside the North American market, with 9,000 dealers in Europe alone. In essence, ADP is the auto dealers' information processing system. Its on-site computers and communications installations assist dealers in all areas of operation: workstations for the customer handling process, links to lenders to speed auto loans, Web sites that connect car shoppers with dealers, and sales data reports and breakdowns.

ADP has everything going for it. It is the leader in its fields. The company has little debt and provides a return on shareholder equity of more than 20 percent. It has increased its dividend every year for a quarter century and maintains a major stock buyback program. It has been cranking out 12 to 14 percent earnings growth for decades, and there is no reason to expect a slowdown. ADP is really a high-tech company without the volatility.

CONTACT INFORMATION:

Automatic Data Processing, Inc.
1 ADP Boulevard
Roseland, NJ 07068
Telephone: (973) 974-5000
www.adp.com

COCA-COLA

The Refreshment Company that Never Pauses

TICKER SYMBOL: KO   EXCHANGE: NYSE

Coca-Cola is the second most widely recognized term in the world, according to one survey, edged out only by "OK."

Coke's achievement is awesome. Almost every year more cases of its drinks are sold and higher profits are reported. How can a company that already sells 1 billion bottles of its drinks a day keep up an expansion record like that? The answer can be found by looking abroad.

Foreign thirsts now account for 70 percent of Coke's sales, 75 percent of its profits, and 90 percent of its earnings growth. Its products are sold in 14 million retail outlets in some 200 countries, accounting for half of the world's soft drink market. It outsells Pepsi, its chief international rival, three to one. In fact, Pepsi has backed away from many foreign markets, knowing it can't compete with the Coke juggernaut. Pepsi got an early toehold in Russia, for example, and was outselling Coke ten to one. Then Coke got serious and spent $650 million on a bottling network that reaches 80 percent of the Russian population. Its volume in Russia is now three times Pepsi's.

Coca-Cola has other drinks besides its namesake. In the U.S. its best-known soft drink brands are Sprite, Fanta, and Nestea. Its Minute Maid unit is one of the world leaders in juice drinks. Coke also distributes bottled water (including the Dasani brand), sports drinks (such as Powerade), and acquired the non-U.S. (excluding France and South Africa) sales rights to the soft drinks of Cadbury Schweppes, adding Canada Dry, Dr. Pepper, Schweppes, and some other labels to its international arsenal. Indeed, the company has hundreds of brands around the globe, with about a dozen new ones introduced every year.

Coke outsells the leading tea in Britain, the leading bottled water in France, and the leading coffee in Brazil. As management guru Peter Drucker has commented, Coke is "a symbol of the way of life most people in the world aspire to."

Coca-Cola wholly owns few bottling plants. Instead, it sells its concentrates to independent bottlers, which vastly lowers the company's capital needs. It routinely takes an equity position in these bottling operations and consolidates a portion of their earnings into its own. This arrangement is one reason for the company's remarkable gross profit margins. Coke's management is relentlessly driven to sell more product by reaching new stores in remote villages, placing vending machines in additional college dorms, and getting exclusive contracts from yet more restaurant chains (it already has McDonald's and Burger King sewed up).

Outside the U.S., the potential for growth is virtually unlimited. Coke may sell 1 billion servings of its products each day, but the world consumes 47 billion servings of *other* beverages. This means there's plenty of opportunity still ahead. As the company is fond of saying, if every person in the world drank one more serving of its products every day, unit case volume would go up 600 percent.

Coke's future growth is more apt to approach rather than exceed the 15 percent-plus annual rates of the past. But no other name comes to mind as being more likely to remain a solid growth company 10, 20, or even 30 years out. Coca-Cola is a core stock for your nest egg.

CONTACT INFORMATION:
The Coca-Cola Company
1 Coca-Cola Plaza
Atlanta, GA 30313
Telephone: (404) 676-2121
www.cocacola.com

COLGATE-PALMOLIVE

A Missionary Zeal

TICKER SYMBOL: CL   EXCHANGE: NEW YORK

Colgate-Palmolive's growth is a case history in the magnification power of globalization. Few companies have been expanding abroad as long and determinedly as Colgate. It now sells tooth-brushes, toothpastes, toiletries, detergents, and other household products in more than 200 countries. Nearly 70 percent of its revenues come from foreign operations, with more than 50 per-cent from the emerging markets. (The company prefers to call them "high-growth markets," for they are indeed providing the company's fastest growth.)

Latin America alone, where Colgate is number one in sales of toothpastes, stick deodorants, fabric softeners, cleansers, and dishwashing products, accounts for about one-quarter of the company's revenues. Its toothbrushes and toothpastes are also the top sellers in most Asian countries, and its shampoos are now available in more than 80 percent of Russia.

You don't achieve that kind of dominance merely by show-ing up and planting a flag. Colgate's management has skillfully built brand recognition and distribution channels around the world. Perhaps no effort has been more ambitious than Colgate's dental-care mobile clinics that travel to even remote villages to demonstrate proper tooth-brushing techniques and leave behind samples of Colgate brushes and pastes. In India, for example, where people use 67 grams of toothpaste a year against the worldwide average of 362 grams, Colgate's mobile clinics visit some 16,000 villages a year, reaching an estimated 15 million potential loyal customers. Worldwide, about double that number of children (through school programs) and their parents are con-tacted annually.

The Colgate name is bannered everywhere, but adaptations are made to cater to local markets. Lower-priced brands, smaller packages, and refill packs are promoted in poorer countries. An Ajax cleanser with an insect-repellent additive has been a big seller in humid climates. Fabric softeners are given one fragrance in France, and a different one in Greece.

Distributors in more than two dozen countries have received special training and software to make it profitable for them to sign up the smallest mom-and-pop shops. Colgate products, for example, are now distributed to 90 percent of Vietnam's retail outlets.

Many initiatives are inspired by consumer research. More than 500,000 shoppers in over 30 countries are interviewed annually to find out what they really want in the way of household and personal-care products. Colgate's laboratories and marketers then cooperate to create responses. Hundreds of new products are introduced every year. Products that didn't exist five years ago now account for about one-third of Colgate's sales.

New products that gain acceptance in one market can then be introduced in others. Protex antibacterial bar soap, first sold in Central America, is now available in more than 40 countries. Colgate Total, a medicinal toothpaste introduced in 1992 that fights gingivitis as well as plaque and cavities, is now sold in more than 100 countries. Hill's Prescription Diet pet food is sold in over 95 percent of U.S. veterinary hospitals, but is also distributed in more than 60 countries, making it the world leader in specialty pet food.

The company says that about two-thirds of its potential population lives in developing countries. Colgate is determined to be a leader in those markets, while maintaining the stronghold it already has in the United States.

CONTACT INFORMATION:

Colgate-Palmolive Company
300 Park Avenue
New York, NY 10022
Telephone: (212) 310-2000
www.colgate.com

DISNEY (WALT) COMPANY

A Mouse that Roars

TICKER SYMBOL: DIS   EXCHANGE: NYSE

Entertainment is a booming industry around the world. As soon as people have a little discretionary income, they think about a television, a night at the movies, or days at a resort. In a global context, Disney practically owns entertainment.

In addition to its animated and live-action movies, Disney is a powerhouse in both network and cable television broadcasting, with ABC, the Disney Channel, ESPN, Lifetime, A&E, and the History Channel among its stable. On the Internet, Disney offers ESPN Sports Zone, ABC News, and Disney's Blast for children.

Then there are the theme parks, including those outside Tokyo and Paris (the latter struggled at first but now attracts twice as many paid visitors as the Eiffel Tower). When the People's Republic of China came to select Disney as the sponsor of a new theme park to be developed in Hong Kong, there just wasn't a realistic alternative.

The live theater performances, first *Beauty and the Beast*, followed by the enormously successful *The Lion King*, and now Elton John and Tim Rice's *Aida*, have been enormously successful. Publishing, home video, computer programs and games, records, and merchandise licensing, not to mention resorts, convention sites, local television and radio stations, and passenger cruise ships round out the mix.

What's more, Disney stores, supplemented by "product corners" in department stores and other outlets, sell Disney memorabilia. Disney has been outstanding in using and leveraging high-tech and creating synergies for its various business units.

The company is four times the size it was a decade ago. Some of this growth was generated from new concepts, such as cruise ships. But growth also comes from the expansion of existing franchises. Disney World's Magic Kingdom opened in 1971 with 1,808 hotel rooms; now there are more than 25,000 rooms, with three additional theme parks—Epcot Center, Disney-MGM Studios, and Disney's Animal Kingdom. There are also evening entertainment centers, convention halls, water parks, a sports complex, and six golf courses in the Orlando area alone. Disney's California Adventure, adjacent to Disneyland in Anaheim, opened in 2001, as did DisneySea, a brand new park next to Tokyo Disneyland.

The Disney complex of enterprises defines synergy. When a new animated film is released, previews appear on the Disney Channel, trailers on TV monitors in the stores, tie-in merchandise at McDonald's, billboards and posters at the parks, specials on ABC, features in *Disney Magazine*, and the film's music on affiliated radio networks. Few parents will not be informed by their offspring that a must-see film has arrived.

Beauty and the Beast troupes are touring Europe, Asia, and Latin America. ESPN is shown in more than 150 countries in twenty languages. There are Disney Stores in some one dozen countries. About one-quarter of the company's revenues now come from overseas, and that number is growing.

Although I still include Disney among The Trusty 20, I have not been a holder since early 1998. The deceleration in its 20 percent compound annual growth rate that I anticipated following its merger with Capital Cities/ABC has been even sharper than I earlier envisioned. Disney has not been immune to the erosion in profitability of network television, losers have been more frequent than winners among its non-animated films, Disney's retail stores have had to be reformatted, and the weak economy—exacerbated by the incident of September 11—have all taken their toll. Most of these are cyclical and temporary in nature and will be reversed. Moreover, the non-business cycle-related problems are fixable and have not impaired this great global growth franchise. DIS will undoubtedly be back in the core portfolio someday.

CONTACT INFORMATION:

The Walt Disney Company
500 South Buena Vista Street
Burbank, CA 91521
Telephone: (818) 560-1000
www.disney.com

THE GILLETTE COMPANY
King of the Disposables

TICKER SYMBOL: G   EXCHANGE: NYSE

It is extraordinary how Gillette manages to apply advanced technology to the lowly razor. Since the 1970s Gillette has provided men with ever closer and gentler shaves with Trac II, Atra, Sensor, SensorExcel, and the latest generation Mach3 (for which the company was awarded some 35 patents), and Venus for women. As a result of these successively perfected systems, Gillette controls more than 70 percent of the wet-shave market in the United States and Europe, 80 percent in China, and 91 percent in Latin America.

Gillette epitomizes the virtues I look for in a growth company. Not only does its near-monopoly of the shaving market give it pricing flexibility, thus assuring healthy profit margins, but by continually introducing more sophisticated versions of its products it can also command ever-higher prices. Mach3 cartridges, for example, cost about 35 percent more than the SensorExcel version.

Though razors and blades—including highly successful shaving lines for women—account for 40 percent of Gillette's sales and one-half of its profits, the company has many other products to sell the world. There are after-shave lotions, deodorants, skin creams, and the Oral-B line of toothbrushes and other oral care products to complete the morning's grooming routine. Gillette's Duracell unit is the world leader in alkaline batteries.

Gillette's product line-up may seem disparate, but consider this: You can go into any convenience store and buy razor blades, a toothbrush, deodorant, and batteries. What they have in common is they are relatively inexpensive consumer items that must continually be replaced. Some 1.2 billion people around the world use at least one Gillette product daily (up from 800 million in 1990).

Gillette gathers about two-thirds of its sales outside the United States. It is a pioneer in international operations, having opened a sales office in India in 1919. Its razors and blades are now sold in some 200 countries. The infrastructure is in place to extend the distribution of the company's other items.

Gillette has experienced some growing pains of late, and has taken steps to address them, including hiring a new CEO. The problems were centered in the battery business and not due to competition in the core blade franchise, where the company's market share has actually increased.

Business Week has called Gillette "one of the consumer world's great innovation machines." Expenditures on research and development, as a percentage of sales, are one of the highest of any consumer products company. And only Coca-Cola among major consumer products companies has realized higher operating profit margins. Although Gillette's momentum has been temporarily interrupted, the company remains one of the world's great unfolding growth stories.

CONTACT INFORMATION:

The Gillette Company
Prudential Tower Building
Boston, MA 02199
Telephone: (617) 421-7000
www.gillette.com

HOME DEPOT

Building the Future

TICKER SYMBOL: HD   EXCHANGE: NYSE

Since its founding in 1978, Home Depot has become not only the world's largest home improvement retailer, but also one of the country's largest retailers of any kind. The company's potential to do the same globally is huge and only in the early stages of being exploited. Home Depot entered Canada in 1994 and quickly dominated the do-it-yourself market there. Expansion into Latin America has already begun. Europe and Asia will be next.

Giant discount superstores have been the retailing blockbusters of recent times, just as the mall was the great innovation of the post-war years. Home Depot combines warehouse prices with an enormous selection—40,000 to 50,000 items—along with salespeople trained and knowledgeable enough to be truly helpful to customers looking for specific building materials, home improvement items, and lawn and garden supplies.

Do-it-yourselfers are the bulk of Home Depot's market, but management also has its sights set on an even bigger market—professional builders, contractors, property maintenance managers, electricians, plumbers, landscapers, and interior designers. The total do-it-yourself market is estimated to be about $100 billion a year, but Home Depot pegs its potential slice of the professional market at more than twice that amount. Many of its stores now cater to professionals by offering earlier operating hours, job-lot quantities of high-demand items, onsite credit, special service desks and checkout counters, and additional delivery options. The company has also acquired several direct mail services whose catalogs go mainly to professionals.

Home Depot has high expectations as well from its series of EXPO Design Centers, which feature design and decorating consulting, products, and installation services for those undertaking serious, big-ticket home decorating and remodeling projects, with no desire to do the work on their own. The logistics of operating an expanding chain of stores are obviously formidable, though management, armed with information technology, has proved its mettle. Continuous review of sales patterns leads to concentration on areas that are more profitable. In terms of per-unit sales volume, profits to sales per square foot, profitability per store, and other measures, Home Depot beats its rivals hands down.

Size in itself brings advantages. High sales volume means tough bargaining sessions with suppliers. The stores are large enough to take direct deliveries, lowering the need for distribution centers. Home Depot is also big enough to develop private brands and undertake much of its own importing, eliminating middlemen.

Demand projections are almost unanimously favorable to Home Depot's future. Housing turnover has been running at the highest rate in history, and new owners invariably want to make improvements and customize to personal tastes. Baby boomers are trading up and buying vacation homes. More minorities and immigrants are buying homes. In fact, studies show that over the next 10 years, an average of 1.2 million new households will be formed annually in the United States. The available housing inventory is aging. By 2010, one-quarter of American homes will be at least 50 years old. This has to translate into rising outlays for maintenance and repairs.

Wherever Home Depot builds, it proves a tough competitor. Domestic growth of around 20 percent a year is projected for the foreseeable future. Overseas expansion would only solidify those expectations.

CONTACT INFORMATION:

The Home Depot, Inc.
2455 Paces Ferry Road
Atlanta, GA 30339-4024
Telephone: (770) 433-8211
www.homedepot.com

JOHNSON & JOHNSON

Health Care Giant

TICKER SYMBOL: JNJ   EXCHANGE: NYSE

For most of us, the name Johnson & Johnson brings to mind Band-Aids, baby powder, and Tylenol. The company's myriad of consumer products are indeed known and respected around the world. But J&J is far more than a maker of drugstore staples. It is one of the world's major pharmaceutical and medical supply companies.

Its drugs, prescribed worldwide, are used to treat everything from bronchitis to anemia, epilepsy to schizophrenia. Its various units make angioplasty stents, intravenous catheters, joint implants, and a host of diagnostic, surgical, and treatment aids. J&J spends more than $2 billion a year on research—the outlay has more than doubled over the past 10 years—placing it among the top 10 companies in the United States in terms of research budgets. When it comes to health care, the company claims "no company on earth can match the diversity and breadth of products and services" that J&J provides.

Johnson & Johnson is also respected for expanding its product line through astute acquisitions. In 2001, the company acquired drug delivery specialist Alza, which gives it expertise that should help expand the possible applications for current J&J drugs that are due to go off patent. Alza's technologies include OROS (to deliver drugs orally), D-TRANS (to deliver drugs transdermally), and ALZAMER (to deliver small molecule drugs by injection). J&J became the second largest biotechnology company in the world when it acquired Centocor in 1999 and integrated it with its Ortho Biotech subsidiary.

Other acquisitions include Cordis, a major name in cardiovascular treatment (it is the market leader in stents and angioplasty balloons); Neutrogena, the popular maker of skin care products; and DePuy, Inc., a manufacturer of orthopedic devices, thus making J&J the leader in artificial joints. Hip, knee, and other joint replacements are now a $4 billion market globally. J&J also keeps its new product pipeline full through 125 to 150 third-party transactions annually, such as research collaborations and licensing arrangements, plus investments in start-up and smaller pharmaceutical firms with promising projects.

Everyday consumer health and grooming aids are also contributing to global growth. In addition to its universally known first-aid, baby, and skin care lines, J&J is a leading maker of non-prescription drugs to treat colds, allergies, and sinus conditions; pain relievers (such Motrin and Tylenol); toiletries; vitamins; toothbrushes; feminine hygiene products; and specialty items such as nicotine withdrawal patches and Lactaid products for the lactose-intolerant. J&J's Acuvue is the number one brand of disposable contact lenses. In 1989, the company formed a 50/50 joint venture with Merck: J&J distributes non-prescription products derived from Merck's prescription medicines. The partnership's biggest successes have been the antacids Mylanta and Pepcid.

Organizationally, Johnson & Johnson is decentralized, with more than 190 operating companies, each focusing on its own market. This has proved highly effective at managing and promoting growth. International business now accounts for about half of total revenues. Cash flow has been generous enough to cover the cost of acquisitions, leaving the company with virtually no debt, while still permitting regular dividend increases. Costs are tightly controlled, and various reengineering initiatives have saved billions in annual operating expenses.

J&J's product line is broad and dynamic enough to sustain annual earnings-per-share growth of 13 to 14 percent for the foreseeable future. Further global expansion could prove that figure to be rather modest.

CONTACT INFORMATION:

Johnson & Johnson
1 Johnson & Johnson Plaza
New Brunswick, NJ 08933
Telephone: (732) 524-0400
www.jnj.com

MARRIOTT INTERNATIONAL
Innkeeper to a World on the Move

TICKER SYMBOL: MAR   EXCHANGE: NYSE

Once you agree that we have entered an era of rising world prosperity, you must be bullish on the hotel industry. One of the first satisfactions of a higher income is travel. A global economy assures a never-ending torrent of business travelers. Hospitality, therefore, has to be a growth business.

Marriott International is the largest operator and franchiser of hotels and resorts in the world, with more than 2,100 locations in 60 countries. Additional operations include timeshare and retirement community development. The company evolved from the 1993 split of the old Marriott Corporation, in which the highly leveraged and capital intensive hotel ownership business (Host Marriott Corporation) was separated from the hotel management business.

With 21 distinct brands and businesses, Marriott offers the broadest and arguably strongest portfolio of hospitality brands in the world. Major brands include Ritz Carlton, Renaissance, Residence Inn, Fairfield Inn, and Courtyard, in addition to the company's namesake. Marriott's powerful brands, built on a long-standing reputation of quality products and services, provide both a strong competitive advantage and pricing flexibility. This is evidenced by Marriott's ability to generate revenues per available room that are up to 35 percent higher than those of its direct competitors.

The company's brands hold leading positions in the premium segment of the hospitality market, but go far beyond that. Marriott's strategy is to offer a wide variety of high quality lodging products at various price points by offering something for just about everyone.

The strength of the company's brands and resulting superior financial returns of Marriott hotels—thanks to higher occupancy rates and premium pricing—also provide significant incentives to owners of competing hotel brands to convert over to Marriott. Over the past several years, approximately 25 percent of all guest rooms added to the company's portfolio were a result of conversions from competing brands. Competition in the lodging industry outside of the United States is highly fragmented and comes primarily from independent operators.

Marriott also benefits from its high-tech reservation system, which refers customers to other brands within the Marriott family if the initial property requested is full. The ability to cross-sell effectively results in more efficient occupancy management, along with costs per reservation that are below the industry average. In addition, Marriott Rewards is the most successful awards program in the lodging industry, resulting in high customer loyalty.

Another important competitive advantage results from the fact that Marriott actually owns very few hotels, opting instead to focus on management and franchising fees. As a result, the business is less exposed to the cyclical nature of the hotel industry, which is often at the mercy of fluctuations in the economy. This strength was amply demonstrated in the wake of the September 11, 2001 terrorist attack that negatively impacted the travel and lodging industries.

The company's corporate goal is "to create significant value by aggressively building its brands and growing its business. The company is dedicated to providing exceptional service to customers, growth opportunities for associates, and attractive returns to shareholders and owners." Management is confident it can continue to deliver growth in the "high teens." Marriott is a natural addition to your nest egg.

CONTACT INFORMATION:

Marriott International, Inc.
10400 Fernwood Road
Bethesda, MD 20817
Telephone: (301) 380-3000
www.marriott.com

MC DONALD'S

The Sun Never Sets on the Golden Arches

TICKER SYMBOL: MCD   EXCHANGE: NEW YORK

When McDonald's opened its first restaurant in the former Soviet Republic of Minsk in the late 1990s, 4,000 people showed up to eat Big Macs. The police had to be summoned to control the huge crowd. Talk about being popular!

Today, nearly half of McDonald's more than 29,000 restaurants lie outside the United States, generating more than half of the company's operating profits. All locations are customized to comply with local tastes. McDonald's locations in Italy offer pasta dishes; those in Spain serve gazpacho. You can buy Big Macs on many Swiss trains. Japan has more than 4,000 outlets (with teriyaki burgers on the menu), and plans to have 10,000 by the year 2010. China now has several hundred locations, and the number is growing rapidly. Even India has a dozen or so McDonald's, where mutton patties replace beef, augmented by vegetarian choices.

No other restaurant chain even comes close to that kind of global presence, nor is any trying to catch up. McDonald's has added more restaurants around the world in the past five years than its five biggest branded fast-food chain competitors combined. It has lined up partners who know the local terrain and supplied them with site development and operational expertise, along with the famous menu, back-up advertising, and promotional support. McDonald's is a sponsor of the World Cup soccer championships, for example, and one of the International Olympic Committee's worldwide partners. It also has a long-term marketing alliance with another global brand, Disney.

McDonald's promotes Disney movies and is the restaurant of choice for Disney's theme parks.

As with any far-flung enterprise, McDonald's predictably encounters setbacks. But good managements don't go into denial; they fix their problems. Sluggish economies (both in the United States and abroad), unfavorable foreign currency adjustments, and the effects of mad cow and foot and mouth diseases on its overseas business can contribute to temporary lackluster showings. In responding to these challenges, management has decentralized operations and improved its relations with franchisees. Most importantly, the company completely overhauled its food preparation process, installing high-tech kitchens that are faster providers of fresher, hotter food. Additional chicken and fish alternatives—even vegetarian burgers—cater to the health-conscious.

Still, if McDonald's were dependent only on domestic operations, where competition is tough and saturation an eventual issue, investors could well be skeptical about the company's continued growth. Domestically, the company is responding by purchasing additional restaurant concepts, such as Boston Market and Chipotle Mexican grills. But it is the foreign markets that hold such exciting promise. The American habit of satisfying hunger with a burger, fries, and shake is being adopted everywhere, as more and more families can afford a McDonald's meal out, more wives abandon their kitchen stove for an office desk, and competitive pressures eradicate the long, leisurely lunch hour. McDonald's faces far less competition in most foreign countries than it does domestically. China and Russia alone offer vast growth possibilities, and the company foresees exceptional growth upcoming in Mexico, Argentina, Spain, Poland, and South Africa as well.

Annual sales per unit abroad are higher than domestically and so are profit margins. Every day some 45 million people visit a

McDonald's, but that's still less than 1 percent of the world's population. The Big Mac still has plenty of new worlds to conquer.

CONTACT INFORMATION:

McDonald's Corporation
McDonald's Plaza
Oak Brook, IL 60523
Telephone: (630) 623-3000
www.mcdonalds.com

MERCK

A Curative Arsenal

TICKER SYMBOL: MRK   EXCHANGE: NYSE

The human body is vulnerable to the same afflictions no matter where you live. Therefore, any ameliorative drug can be prescribed universally. Merck is a global pharmaceutical company that generates about 40 percent of its profits outside of the United States. Through its focus on research and development, and its strategy to generate the best science for every research and development dollar invested, the company discovers, develops, manufactures, and markets a broad range of human health products and services.

Five products are key to Merck's recent growth and account for about 60 percent of the company's sales. These are Vioxx for osteoarthritis and acute pain; Zocor for cholesterol; Cozaar and Hyzaar for high blood pressure; Fosamax for osteoporosis; and Singulair for asthma. The enormous success of these medications should be prolonged and enhanced by new indications for each drug that are currently in various stages of review by the FDA.

Although several products that had paced past growth have been coming off patent, the combination of new medicines, in-development products, and R&D productivity should more than offset the effects of these expirations. More products are in the development pipeline than ever before in the company's history, including treatments for fungal and a multitude of other infections, depression, nausea associated with chemotherapy, shingles, diabetes, and HIV/AIDS. These healing compounds are refined in eight major research centers throughout the United States, Europe, and Japan. To complement Merck's internal research programs, the company has formed collaborations with more than 40 companies, institutes, and universities around the world.

Merck is also a leading developer and distributor of vaccines. Its M-M-R II, a combination vaccine for the prevention of measles, mumps, and rubella, is estimated to have prevented tens of thousands of deaths since 1978. Other vaccines are aimed at preventing hepatitis and chicken pox. Another division turns out animal drugs. Ivermectin, a parasecticide, is the biggest selling animal health product in the world. Crop protection agents also emerge from Merck's labs.

The company operates Merck-Medco, which provides pharmaceutical benefit services to more than 65 million people. Operations from Merck-Medco are responsible for about half of the company's total revenues in recent years, and have been growing at more than 30 percent a year. Merck-Medco.com is the world's leading Internet pharmacy, processing more than 110,000 prescriptions per week via the Internet.

In 2000, Merck-Medco launched two important initiatives to help address rising pharmaceutical costs: Generics First is an effort to educate physicians and consumers about the appropriate use of generic medications. YOURx Plan, created in association with Reader's Digest, is a pharmacy discount program for people without adequate prescription drug insurance coverage.

No other pharmaceutical company is better positioned than Merck to capitalize on any expansion of prescription drug benefits for the elderly. Merck represents a powerhouse core holding in almost any long-term financial plan.

CONTACT INFORMATION:

Merck & Co., Inc.
1 Merck Drive
Whitehouse Station, NJ 08889-0100
Telephone: (908) 423-1000
www.merck.com

PFIZER

Research Juggernaut

TICKER SYMBOL: PFE   EXCHANGE: NYSE

One year after celebrating its 150th year in operation, Pfizer merged with Warner-Lambert in 2000, becoming the world's largest and fastest growing major pharmaceutical company. The merger not only gave the company Lipitor, the leading cholesterol-lowering drug with sales of more than $5 billion, but also boosted its research capabilities. Pfizer Global Research and Development has an annual budget of about $5 billion and is the largest operation of its kind in the world, boasting some 12,000 researchers at centers on three continents.

Pfizer has eight human pharmaceutical products that ring up annual sales of $1 billion or more. In addition to Lipitor, these include Viagra for erectile dysfunction; Zoloft, an anti-depressant; Neurontin, the world's leading epilepsy medicine; Celebrex, a co-leader with Merck in the market for non-steroidal, anti-inflammatory medications; Zithromax, the biggest selling antibiotic in its class; Diflucan, the world's leading prescription anti-fungal product; and Norvasc, the once-a-day medication for high blood pressure and heart pain.

Overall, Pfizer has well more than 150 research projects underway targeting all of the major disease categories. Pfizer's product pipeline is relatively young and stable, with significant patent protection. (Most of its blockbusters won't be coming off patent until 2004–2013.)

Another outstanding strength is Pfizer's worldwide sales force. At 4,500 strong, it is the industry's largest. Other pharmaceutical houses look to Pfizer when seeking a partner to gain wider distribution. For example, Lipitor was originally marketed by Pfizer under an agreement with developer Warner-Lambert until the two companies merged. Eisai, a Japanese company that entered into a joint arrangement with Pfizer, developed Aricept, used in treating Alzheimer's. And Pfizer worked with G.D. Searle, a division of Monsanto Chemical, to co-develop and co-promote Searle's Celebrex treatment for arthritis.

Though pharmaceuticals account for three-quarters of its revenues, Pfizer does make over-the-counter consumer products. In addition, its animal health products division, with vaccines and medications for both livestock and household pets, is one of the world's largest.

In recent years, Pfizer's sales have grown twice as fast as the industry's. Earnings per share have risen more than 20 percent annually and dividends have been raised for more than 30 consecutive years.

Pfizer is continually expanding its global presence, with overseas markets already accounting for 40 percent of sales.

The future is definitely bright for this company that has a very strong position in what is, and is bound to remain, a rapidly growing industry.

CONTACT INFORMATION:

Pfizer, Inc.
235 E. 42nd Street
New York, NY 10017-5755
Telephone: (212) 573-2323
www.pfizer.com

STAPLES

Taking Care of Business

TICKER SYMBOL: SPLS   EXCHANGE: NASDAQ

Though its first emporium only opened in 1986, Staples is now the world's largest operator of office product superstores, with no signs of slowing down. The company, headquartered in Boston, pioneered the office superstore concept.

Rapid expansion accounts for most of the company's fast success. Staples has been opening well over 100 stores a year, with more than 1,300 stores now in the United States, Canada, the United Kingdom, Germany, and Portugal. Sales growth in existing stores has been vigorous, driven by a solid economy, the proliferation of small businesses and home offices, and new and improved technologies that create must-have office tools.

Only skilled and disciplined management could handle this measure of growth. Staples' chiefs are acknowledged to be the best in the industry. Its same-store sales consistently outpace those of rivals. New store proposals are subjected to the strictest return-based analysis. Constant remodeling keeps stores fresh and bright. Shelving configurations and merchandise assortments are periodically revamped to optimize returns per square foot. When copy centers proved more profitable than furniture, for example, the centers were expanded at the expense of the latter.

Information systems are state-of-the-art. Buyers exploit global product sourcing to keep prices low. Regional warehouses allow stores to maintain just-in-time inventories. And Staples has built a brand image for its own name sufficient to permit stocking an increasing variety of higher-margin private-label products.

Staples superstores offer some 7,000 items, and are primarily geared toward small and medium-size businesses. But Staples isn't just a chain of superstores. Smaller stores (called Staples Express) in towns with lower populations, and multiple locations in large cities, have proved highly profitable. Its catalogs also reach customers in tinier markets. The company has built a major business supplying large corporations, under contract, with all their office needs. Staples is also a big player on the Internet.

When Staples first added its catalog business back in 1989, the company learned that customers who shop both by catalog and in person spend twice as much than those who visit the stores alone. Those who shop by catalog, in person, and on the company's Website spend 4.5 times as much as store-only customers. To encourage this multi-channel migration, and to present a broader product selection, the company rolled out Internet kiosks in all U.S. stores, offering a wealth of information. More than 100,000 products are offered online.

Management has stated that its goal is a continuation of 20 percent sales growth and a higher rate of earnings-per-share growth. Office product expenditures in the United States are growing at a 10 percent rate, and Staples still has less than a 5 percent share of this highly fragmented market. Moreover, North America isn't the world. The European Common Market, in fact, is a larger potential market, which Staples is going after in a major way.

Getting down to business in a capitalistic age throughout the world is very profitable, and arguably no one does it better than Staples.

CONTACT INFORMATION:

Staples, Inc.
500 Staples Drive
Framingham, MA 01702
Telephone: (508) 253-5000
www.staples.com

STARBUCKS

Cupbearer to the Masses

TICKER SYMBOL: SBUX   EXCHANGE: NASDAQ

Starbucks is more than the country's leading purveyor of specialty coffees; it is a phenomenon. Starbucks conjures up images of urbanity, quality, and an oasis where a few dollars buys a special break.

Moreover, it manages to convey exclusivity without being exclusive. A new Starbucks is born at the rate of about one a day.

The first Starbucks opened in Seattle's Pike Place Market in 1971. Legendary chairman Howard Schultz joined the company as director of retail operations and marketing in 1982. A year later, he traveled to Italy and was impressed by the popularity of expresso bars in Milan. When he returned home, he convinced the founders of Starbucks to test the concept of coffee bars at another location in downtown Seattle. The rest is history.

The company eventually went public in 1992, and now has close to 5,000 locations worldwide, and growing. This includes the full-sized shops, along with the smaller kiosks in airports, malls, office lobbies, and through business relationships with Barnes and Noble bookstores, Nordstrom's department stores, Marriott and Sheraton Hotels, and Albertson's supermarkets.

Yet the market is far from saturated. Roughly half of the top 100 markets in this country have yet to be fully tapped.

Then there is the world. In 1998, Starbucks bought a 61-store chain of coffee shops in Britain, which gave it a base from which to expand into Europe. Successful forays are now underway in Switzerland, Italy, and Austria. The taste for coffee in Asia is growing at an even faster rate. Mostly through joint ventures, Starbucks now has stores in Japan, Singapore, South Korea, Taiwan, Thailand, the Philippines, and New Zealand. Overall, the company estimates that it can grow to more than 20,000 stores worldwide.

Growth also comes from new products. Frappuccino, which appeared in 1997, was a brilliant introduction—a cool refreshment for the months when hot coffee has less appeal. It was followed a year later by Tazzi, an icy mixture of tea and juice. Starbucks ice cream (a joint venture with Dreyers) and bottled Frappaccino (with PepsiCo as a partner) have proved big hits in supermarkets and convenience stores. Now they are being joined by bins of Starbucks packaged coffee beans, commanding the same premium price as in the company's shops. Mail-order and Internet business for coffee and merchandise—from mugs to cappuccino machines—is accelerating.

Starbucks has so much in its favor. It enjoys a dominant position in a fast-growing global market. Repeat business is a given. So is its reputation for quality. The company motivates its employees, including qualified part-timers, with above-average wages, benefits, and stock options. Company management has projected annual earnings growth of about 20 percent for years to come.

How will they do it? By continuing to rapidly expand retail operations, growing specialty sales and other operations, and selectively pursuing opportunities to leverage the Starbucks brand through the introduction of new products and the development of new distribution channels.

Given the company's unsurpassed passion, and demonstrated ability to come up with innovative merchandising concepts, there's no reason they shouldn't continue to succeed.

CONTACT INFORMATION:

Starbucks Corporation
2401 Utah Avenue South
Seattle, WA 98134
Telephone: (206) 447-1575
www.starbucks.com

STATE STREET CORP.

Keeper of the World's Wealth

TICKER SYMBOL: STT   EXCHANGE: NYSE

State Street Corp. was founded as a traditional bank in 1792. Having sold off the last of its pure banking activities in 1999, the company now concentrates on investment services, which account for 80 percent of revenues. The remaining 20 percent comes from investment management. State Street calls itself "a specialist in serving institutional investors," meaning pension funds, endowments, foundations, insurance companies, and mutual funds.

An early and still key activity for the company is serving as custodian for the assets banks and other intermediaries manage. This involves the safekeeping of securities; accounting for buys, sells, dividends, and interest payments; assigning a daily value to portfolios; updating all records; and keeping the institutions current on their holdings. Since institutions have increasingly invested internationally, State Street has developed the capability of handling transactions in some 40 different currencies. The latest count shows that State Street is custodian to more than $6 trillion in assets. It is far and away the largest service provider for U.S. mutual funds, which has been an obvious engine of growth in recent years.

State Street now does far more than custodial work, and keeps adding new services all the time. For example, it handles the record keeping, administration, and employee communications for 401(k) plans. It checks money managers' compliance with the contractual investment guidelines between pension fund sponsors. It consolidates multi-currency reports into a single-currency document to simplify reporting of investment results.

Increasingly, State Street has been moving beyond caretaker and oversight jobs into performance-enhancing products and tools for those who manage portfolios. It invests cash balances, arranges securities lending, handles foreign exchange trading, takes care of transaction settlement and clearing, provides customized reports and analysis of portfolios, and offers data to help managers make investment decisions in the first place. State Street is committed to "serve institutional investors, in any currency, at every stage of the investment process, anywhere in the world."

State Street has both helped make globalization a reality and profited from its spread. It now has offices in 23 countries serving clients in some 60 countries, performing the same services it originally developed for U.S. institutions. About one-quarter of the bank's revenues are now derived from non-U.S. customers, and the percentage is rising steadily toward management's goal of 40 percent.

Furthermore, State Street has become a major global investment institution in its own right. It offers active management, but its specialty is indexing.

Information technology is critical to almost every aspect of its businesses. Early on, State Street made a commitment to spend whatever it took to maintain state-of-the-art computer and communications systems. Accordingly, State Street has become one of the world's leading users and developers of technology.

State Street's earnings per share have been rising at a double-digit rate for two decades. It's hard to see how the pace could slow. After all, billions of dollars have poured into mutual funds in the United States, as aging baby boomers stashed money away for their retirement years. The same is happening in other countries. Worldwide, companies are setting up 401(k)-type plans, and governments are either privatizing their pension systems, or considering the move. These trends mean more assets under institutional management, and State Street's fees, calculated as a percentage of those assets, will keep rising. State Street will continue to be a prime beneficiary of the Golden Age of Capitalism.

CONTACT INFORMATION:

State Street Corporation
225 Franklin Street
Boston, MA 02110
Telephone: (617) 786-3000
www.statestreet.com

TIFFANY & CO.

World Class Elegance

TICKER SYMBOL: TIF   EXCHANGE: NYSE

"Tiffany" is a brand that has become synonymous with quality. Likewise, Tiffany & Co. has developed the rare and inestimable image of being a purveyor of fine goods, notable for their design and execution.

Such auras are not created overnight. Tiffany was founded in 1837, in time for Abraham Lincoln to buy his wife a Tiffany pearl necklace. Tiffany artists designed the Belmont Cup, a set of White House china, and pieces now displayed in major museums. The jeweler has served royalty, celebrities, and the super rich. Anyone receiving a gift in that signature baby-blue box anticipates the best. The retailer has been elevated to the status of an institution.

But all this would mean little to investors if Tiffany were still just one grand store on Fifth Avenue, with a few scattered satellites. Only in the past decade has new management taken measured but aggressive steps to leverage the Tiffany name in order to capture a larger market and profits without sacrificing its lofty reputation. There are now more than 100 Tiffany stores and boutiques worldwide, double the number in 1990, as well as Tiffany counters in select jewelry and department stores. In addition, the company has developed a considerable business in direct sales to the public, through catalogs and the Internet, and to companies needing employee incentive awards and customer gifts.

Nearly half of the company's revenues now come from abroad, for Tiffany has evolved into a name that is respected around the world. Including its own stores and wholesale sales to other retailers, Tiffany's goods are available in more than 50 countries.

Tiffany's largest overseas presence is in Japan, where it boasts some 44 stores. Through arrangements with retailer Mitsukoshi Limited, Tiffany goods have been sold in Japan since 1972. Japan now accounts for about 25 percent of Tiffany's profits, and growth has been robust even during the recent years of a sagging economy. The company also has outlets in other parts of the Pacific Rim, including Hong Kong, Singapore, Taiwan, Indonesia, and the Philippines, along with Australia and New Zealand. Tiffany further has a handful of stores in Europe and Latin America. Wherever it's located, Tiffany is widely recognized as a symbol of Western luxury and chic, and the place where the newly arrived aspire to shop.

Adding additional outlets isn't Tiffany's sole strategy for growth. In a fairly stodgy industry, it has proved innovative in both product development and marketing. Offerings are kept broad and diverse, with prices at all levels. Jewelry accounts for nearly three-quarters of sales volume. The balance comes from watches, clocks, china, crystal, silverware, and writing instruments. Constant new designs freshen the stores and catalogs. Tiffany has been particularly adept at collections built around a theme. Its Atlas collection, inspired by the clock in its New York store, has stretched to more than 70 items that can be showcased and promoted.

Obviously, during economic downturns and turmoil in key markets such as Asia, Tiffany will lose incremental business. But its core business is solid. People are always getting engaged and celebrating special occasions, and somehow luxury goods sell even in recessions. After all, the rich are forever with us. Besides, with an average ticket of less than $200, it's not only the rich who can afford to give the blue box. Over the long run, rising world-wide affluence in capitalism's Golden Age bodes well for Tiffany's sterling future.

CONTACT INFORMATION:

Tiffany & Co.
600 Madison Avenue
New York, NY 10022
Telephone: (212) 755-8000
www.tiffany.com

UNITED PARCEL SERVICE

The World's Messenger

TICKER SYMBOL: UPS   EXCHANGE: NYSE

UPS began as a private messenger and delivery service in the Seattle area back in 1907. Today it has evolved into the world's largest express carrier, package deliverer, and a leading global provider of transportation and logistics services. The company's famous brown trucks deliver more than 13 million packages each day to some 6 million customers in more than 200 countries.

The company's mission statement is to be the "world's premier enabler of global commerce." Although UPS competes with postal services run by the United States and other countries, along with a handful of private sector players such as FedEx, Airborne Express, and DHL Worldwide, none enjoy the company's vast scope and reach.

UPS also has a number of other competitive advantages, including its global scale, e-commerce capabilities, broadest range of distribution, and strong culture. The company has an extensive ground and air network, with more than 150,000 vehicles and some 600 aircraft. In addition, unlike its competition, UPS express air services are fully integrated with its ground delivery system, allowing UPS to offer the broadest array of delivery options while maximizing costs. This infrastructure lets UPS reach every U.S. residential and business address. It is also the only company with an integrated air and ground network in Europe, permitting it to offer guaranteed overnight delivery in more than 700 European cities, a breadth unmatched in the industry.

Furthermore, UPS is the largest air cargo and express carrier in Latin America, and is rapidly developing its infrastructure with hubs in Tokyo, Hong Kong, and Taiwan. In 2001, the company was awarded direct flight routes between the United States and China, opening up a tremendous market opportunity.

At the core of the UPS network is a sophisticated technology infrastructure, providing customers with total order visibility and improved customer service, receiving, order management, and accounting operations. No other company is better positioned to participate in and facilitate electronic commerce transactions. The company's service options are fully integrated into many Websites, making UPS a true partner in the rapid growth of Internet-based commerce.

The U.S. package delivery option is the foundation of UPS's business, and will likely remain the primary driver of growth for the foreseeable future. The company's domestic strategy is to leverage its impressive competitive advantages in distribution to cross-sell existing and new services, such as logistics (managing the movement of parts and products between suppliers, production facilities, distribution centers, and customers), freight forwarding, and customs brokerage. In addition, UPS continues to focus on international expansion, which offers tremendous opportunities for growth. The international package delivery market is expanding faster than the domestic market, and as global commerce continues to increase, that trend is unlikely to abate anytime soon.

UPS has a strong culture built on a long history of customer service, reliability, and an "employee-owner" concept. Most employees own stock in the company, a tradition dating back to 1927, although the company has only been publicly traded since 1999.

UPS also benefits from a solid management team and outstanding financial position. Its balance sheet and profitability measures are the strongest among the major transportation com-

panies, and it's not unreasonable to expect superior earnings per
share growth for many years to come.

CONTACT INFORMATION:

United Parcel Service, Inc.
55 Glenlake Parkway NE
Atlanta, GA 30328
Telephone: (404) 828-6000
www.ups.com

WAL-MART

All the World Loves a Bargain

TICKER SYMBOL: WMT   EXCHANGE: NYSE

The little discount store that Sam Walton opened in Rogers, Arkansas in 1962 has evolved into the largest retailer in the world. About 60 million people visit a Wal-Mart store every single week. Over a year, nearly $600 is spent in a Wal-Mart for every man, woman, and child in America.

But that is history. With about 4,000 Wal-Mart discount stores, Sam's Clubs, and Supercenters already open for business in the United States, how can Wal-Mart possibly keep growing?

One answer is the Supercenters, which combine general merchandise with groceries and services such as hair salons, optical centers, and a bank. These bigger stores are more profitable. Wal-Mart has been adding more than 100 a year to the chain, although most of them serve as replacements to the smaller discount stores.

The company is also testing two other types of stores: discount stores half the size of the current stores that can serve smaller communities, and supermarkets (referred to as Neighborhood Markets) that will sell only groceries, drugstore items, and photo processing services. If the Neighborhood Market concept tests well, Wal-Mart says it will go national, extending its lead as the nation's largest food retailer.

The other answer, once again, lies outside the United States. Wal-Mart's first cross-border moves were in North America. In the early 1990s it entered into a joint venture with Mexican retailer Cifra, in which Wal-Mart subsequently acquired a majority interest. Wal-Mart is now Mexico's largest retailer. Then came Canada, with the 1994 purchase of 122 Woolco stores. Within two years, Wal-Mart had 40 percent of the discount market in Canada, twice the share Woolco had managed to capture.

Since then Wal-Marts have opened in Argentina, Brazil, South Korea, China, and Japan. Some are joint ventures; others are go-it-alone operations. Having also entered the European market—with acquisitions in the United Kingdom and Germany—Wal-Mart is well on its way to becoming a global retailer.

Opening faraway markets with stores that carry as many as 50,000 items is not easy and does not come cheap. But once Wal-Mart has six to eight stores in a country, fixed costs are covered. And per-store returns on investment are higher overseas than they are domestically. It was only in 1996, with some 300 stores outside the U.S., that foreign operations turned a profit for the first time. Momentum has been building ever since.

Certainly, the factors that explain Wal-Mart's success are exportable, particularly its ability to undersell competitors because of the quantity of goods it buys from suppliers. It can also export employee loyalty and enthusiasm generated by a gung-ho culture, universal incentive programs (including a profit-sharing plan largely invested in Wal-Mart stock), and the promotions awarded to service its constant growth.

Then there's Wal-Mart's cutting-edge technology. The company spends about $500 million annually on information technology. Its data storage capacity is second only to that of the United States government. Each department manager carries a scanner that lets him or her know how many units of any given item were sold yesterday, last week, and the same period last year; how many are in stock; how many are on the way; and how many are available at the closest Wal-Mart. Ninety million transactions a week are analyzed for clues to merchandising improvements. A "just-in-time" supply system automatically alerts personnel when shelves need restocking. This saves interest and other costs, while assuring item availability and fewer markdowns.

For most investors, most of the time, Wal-Mart should be one of the first eggs added to your nest.

CONTACT INFORMATION:

Wal-Mart Stores, Inc.
702 SW Eighth Street
Bentonville, AR 72716
Telephone: (501) 273-4000
www.walmartstores.com

WRIGLEY (WILLIAM JR.) COMPANY

Satisfying a Universal Craving

TICKER SYMBOL: WWY   EXCHANGE: NYSE

Comfort from chewing must be innate to our species. We know the ancients along the Mediterranean chewed the sweet resin of the mastic tree, a member of the cashew family. For many American Indians, spruce tree resins quenched this need. In tropical countries today, betel nuts, taken from the seeds of betel palms, satisfy the craving.

Americans have considered the name Wrigley practically synonymous with the chewing experience for more than 100 years. Spearmint, Doublemint, and Juicy Fruit are national icons, with the company's comparatively newer brands, Eclipse, Freedent, Big Red, Winterfresh, Hubba Bubba, and sugar-free Extra, gaining similar status. Thirteen of the 14 top-selling gums in the U.S. carry the Wrigley label. But they are no longer American exclusives. The whole world is acquiring the Wrigley habit.

Wrigley's products are consumed daily by millions of people in more than 140 countries. CEO William Wrigley, Jr. took the helm of the company following the death of his father in 1999. He has reenergized the organization and focused resources on growth initiatives, which should result in a further acceleration of the company's growth rate.

The Chicago-based company now has factories in Canada, England, France, Austria, Poland, Australia, the Philippines, Taiwan, India, China, Kenya, and St. Petersburg, Russia. Wrigley's products are sold in more than 140 countries. After all, a stick of chewing gum is a solace almost everyone in the world can afford. Wrigley's overseas business has about doubled over the past five years. Central and Eastern Europe are proving to be highly receptive markets, but the fastest growing area is Asia, especially China. Sales volume in China has grown by at least 50 percent a year since the first factory opened in Guangzhou in 1993—a factory that Wrigley has had to more than double in size. Some 700,000 stores in China now carry Wrigley brands, and the company says it still reaches only about half the population.

It is not as though other countries don't have their indigenous brands. But once again, the American way is the one the world wants to emulate. And Wrigley has been very successful in advertising, promoting, and projecting an image of quality and value. Its brands have become the number one sellers in most of Europe and much of Asia and Latin America, and account for more than half of the world market.

Global expansion is expensive, and the company's capital expenditures—two-thirds of which are overseas—have been high. Still, the company should rack up record sales year after year. Some confections for youngsters—Bubble Tape and Bubble Jug, for example—have helped, but sales growth has mostly been fueled by the consumption of more chewing gum by more of the world's population. This trend is no doubt abetted these days by the desire of millions to quit smoking and take off weight.

The Wrigley Healthcare Division was established in 2001. Its flagship product was Surpass, an antacid chewing gum. Using chewing gum as a fast-acting, good tasting vehicle for the delivery of active ingredients that provide functional health benefits to consumers combines the strength of the company's brand with new technologies to create additional platforms for growth.

Thus, new products and marketing initiatives, coupled with a renewed focus on improving profitability and efficiency, should lead to an acceleration of growth over the next several years. Plus, with its strong financial position, lack of debt, and substantial cash flow, I am convinced that Wrigley can look forward to more assured future growth.

CONTACT INFORMATION:

Wm. Wrigley Jr. Company
410 N. Michigan Avenue
Chicago, IL 60611
Telephone: (312) 644-2121
www.wrigley.com

Chapter Fifteen:
GROWING YOUR GOLDEN AGE NEST EGG

THERE IS ALWAYS ONE MOMENT WHEN THE DOOR OPENS AND LETS
THE FUTURE IN.

GRAHAM GREENE

We have all lived through many of the world events reviewed throughout this book. If there is any surprise in this summary of the familiar, it is the realization of how easy it is to lose sight of the big picture, to fail to grasp just how momentous changes like the collapse of communism in Russia are after 70 years of threat, not to mention the end of the Cold War, the world's conversion from government-manipulated to free markets, the general downsizing of governments, the dismantling of barriers to the flow of goods and capital, the industrialization of so many once somnolent countries, the victory over inflation, and the dazzling achievements of digital technology. Any one of these would be of major importance. Taken together, they have thoroughly shaken up our universe for the better.

Certainly no one laments the end of Soviet power, or denies that hundreds of millions of people around the world have traded poverty for progress and hope. Most understand that technology is a blessing, not a threat. The majority has come to the view that individual responsibility is better than endless cycles of social-welfare dependence, and that free markets offer the best promise of rising living standards for all. The American spirit of self-reliance, opportunity, openness, and optimism has won the world over.

These concurrent and mutually reinforcing dynamics explain what fueled the bull market of the 1990s, and auger its continuation.

Of course, even Golden Ages have tarnished moments. There will be problems, disappointments, and setbacks along the way. We saw a meltdown of the emerging markets in 1997–98, caused by a currency crisis in Asia. The Internet and technology bubble in the United States was followed by a severe overall global market correction in 2000–01. This situation was further complicated by the launching of a war on terrorism that followed the terrorist attacks in late 2001. This exacerbated and extended into 2002 the slowdown in global growth that was already underway. However, I am convinced that President George W. Bush's prayer will be answered and "out of this evil, good will come."

Accordingly I remain steadfast in my belief that we have entered a time of steadily rising world affluence. The changes that have already happened and that are unfolding justify such optimism. The pie is on the table, not in the sky. Even when the economies worldwide soften, it is only a pause in an upward climb. The positive forces are too great and potent to taint the long-term prospects. The future is golden. Patience will be required.

We can expect attempts to turn back the clock—fresh experiments in isolationism, quasi-socialism, and even future acts of terrorism—but they will be contained and relatively short-lived. The world is gradually accepting the truth that cooperation, open borders, political and economic freedom, and unhindered markets open the taps to more wealth for everyone. The twentieth century tried the alternatives, and learned something from the pain.

THE INVESTMENT RESPONSE

A Golden Age means what it says—increasing wealth worldwide. That includes the United States, surely, but also in Europe, Asia, Latin America, and, increasingly, Africa. People everywhere will have more money to spend. Millions upon additional millions will buy goods, restaurant meals, entertainment, and travel experiences they once thought beyond their reach. Doors are opening in many markets, and the companies we have looked at in this book are first in line to prosper. They have the brands and services people know and want; their outlets are being erected around the corner from home; they have the technology to make things happen smoothly; and they are sworn to chase down every last customer. These are the companies investors want on their side. In the environment we have entered, no other strategy is as compelling.

In the business environment unfolding—one without high tariffs, subsidies, and barriers—competition can come from any direction. The number of companies able to command the prices necessary to maintain healthy profit margins will shrink. But if you own the name Coke or Juicy Fruit, Mickey Mouse or Big Mac, Tylenol or Ajax, you can get your target prices, because people want what you have to sell. They want it because they, like everyone else, believe it's the best. To get to the position where a company practically owns a market takes decades, especially in a market that spans the globe. Once a company obtains that hold, it is very difficult to dislodge.

In the 1990s a broad band of corporations reported exceptional earnings growth in the wake of drastic cost-cutting policies. But that process can only go so far. From now on, we'll see the real mettle of companies. We'll know those able to deliver sustainable growth year after year.

Customers who view your store, your service, or your brand as being tops will remain loyal. Repeat business from current customers is a key identifying hallmark of the true growth company, especially when the products and services are relatively impervious to economic conditions. If times are tough, you can usually patch up your old car and drive it another year. But who puts off buying a cold drink on a hot day? Or stops taking allergy pills during hay fever season? Or ignores the family laundry? During the rough patches, people may shop at discount stores (Wal-Mart), eat at restaurants without tablecloths (McDonald's), and become do-it-yourselfers (Home Depot), but they won't go completely without.

Growth companies plow most or all of their profits back into the business to fuel further growth. As we examined earlier, money reinvested—stated as a percentage of a company's equity capital—has proved a good indicator of future earnings progress. The reinvestment rate for The Trusty 20 has historically averaged in the 15 to 20 percent range. The persistent high reinvestment rate of the companies we've reviewed gives me confidence they will keep on reporting high earnings growth going forward. It's also why I believe the performance potential of premier growth companies in the years ahead is the best in my 40 years of professional experience.

CORE CONTENTMENT

There is no such thing as a perfect strategy for all persons and all seasons. However, for the prolonged season ahead, the one I espouse comes close. Any portfolio with companies whose earnings are expanding at a double-digit clip is ideal for those with long-term goals who are eager for growth. One of the beauties of this strategy is that it is at the same time both dynamic and non-speculative.

You can be confident that stocks chosen in accord with this strategy should outperform the S&P 500 because, as in the case with The Trusty 20, the sustainable secular growth rates are well more than twice that of the S&P. That doesn't mean every stock will outpace the S&P each and every year. We have seen that any company can lag for a time before shooting ahead. You, as an investor, must have patience. This can only come from having faith in these companies and taking a long-term view. That, in turn, requires tuning out the siren songs of media pundits, brokers, assorted strategists, locker-room buddies, and your own itch to extrapolate from recent numbers.

Perhaps most meaningful of all to readers of this book is the haven of a portfolio that serves as a solid foundation upon which to build your nest egg. These are not stocks to be traded. One can shut out the daily take-action advice in the press. A portfolio that needs little change is easy on taxes and the psyche. When you own stocks such as Johnson & Johnson, Automatic Data Processing, Abbott Laboratories, Wrigley, United Parcel Service, and Wal-Mart, you can relax. These stocks may suffer intermediate pauses, but you know the bottom is not going to fall out on them, as it did with most Internet stocks. Over the years, these companies will simply go on gathering more sales and profits.

Once you have decided to concentrate your investment portfolio on global leaders, you will rest assured since you no longer need be tempted to take sleep-disturbing risks in small and little understood companies; or feel compelled to spend hours poring over arcane formulas to devise trading schemes; or need to cull through pariah stocks to uncover hidden treasures; or have to reconfigure your portfolio every third month; or find it necessary to check the Dow Jones Industrials at all hours of the day; or fuss about foreign economies and currencies; or quake over the morning headlines and what commentators have to say about them. The wholesale price index may climb, housing starts may fall, and real estate values may collapse in the U.S. None of this matters because your companies are continually conquering new markets.

This strategy is not a get-rich-quickly scheme. Rather, it is a sensible approach for building a solid nest egg over time. Successful investing, like success itself, is a journey, not a destination. The destination will take care of itself. I think you understand that fast-track ambitions usually lead to little more than regret. Options, micro-caps, short-term trading, short-selling, momentum-on-margin, and all the other high-flying gambles are 99 percent guarantees that you will leave the table with empty pockets. Compound your money at a double-digit rate and the wealth will arrive. And the earlier you start, the more you'll have at the end. "Compound interest is the most powerful force in the universe," Albert Einstein once observed.

HE WHO HESITATES LIVES IN REGRET

How long will the Golden Age last? No one can know for sure. History tells us the Silver Age at the end of the last century lasted a good 50 years, though relatively few of the world's population enjoyed its bounty. We can now expect ever-spreading abundance, which will extend global prosperity decade after decade into this new century.

In any case, surmises about the longevity of the good times ahead are irrelevant. If we have decades to go, need investors know or ask for more?

Indeed, it is good to be a long-term investor, but only if you have a good long-term investment plan. I hope you agree that this book gives you the tools you need to put one together. Remember, these are companies to hold, not to trade around. After all, more investment mistakes have been made through a failure to hold on to good companies than from getting out of appreciated securities that are deemed to be "overvalued" by the market. Patience and discipline, based on an unshakable faith in the future, are the hallmarks of a successful investor. Following these principles will lead you to building a solid, long-term, and most profitable nest egg.

ABOUT THE AUTHOR

George M. Yeager is one of the most experienced investment managers on Wall Street and a leader in global growth investing. Yeager is President and Investment Policy Committee Chairman of Yeager, Wood & Marshall, Inc., a New York investment firm. He also manages the U.S. Global Leaders Growth Fund and the U.S. Global Leaders Growth Fund Ltd.

Yeager began his career at the Federal Reserve Bank of New York. He joined his current firm in 1960, and at one time managed a large portion of IBM's pension fund. Yeager, Wood & Marshall has long specialized in growth equity investing, and has concentrated its portfolios exclusively in companies with a global reach since 1989.

Yeager graduated magna cum laude from Dartmouth College, and earned an MBA with high distinction from the Amos Tuck School of Business Administration at Dartmouth. He is a member of numerous professional organizations, including the Association for Investment Management and Research, International Society of Financial Analysts, New York Society of Security Analysts, and is a past governor of the Investment Counsel Association of America.

Yeager is a leading figure in the investment industry, and has been featured in such publications as *Forbes, Fortune, Barron's, Investor's Business Daily, Mutual Funds* magazine, *Financial Planning, Investment Advisor*, and *Financial Advisor Magazine*. His fund has been profiled and recommended in various newsletters and magazines, including *The No-Load Fund Investor, Mutual Fund Monthly*, and Morningstar.com.

Yeager and his wife live in Bronxville, New York. In his spare time, Yeager collects autograph material of American businessmen and financiers, and the art of American impressionist Wilson Irvine.

ORDERING ADDITIONAL BOOKS

If you would like to order additional copies of *Investing Your Nest Egg*, please visit your local bookstore, or go to our official Web site at www.investingyournestegg.com.

INDEX